Mitzi Gaynor

ALSO BY PETER SHELLEY
AND FROM McFARLAND

June Allyson: Her Life and Career (2023)

Brittany Murphy: Her Life and Career (2022)

Ann Miller: Her Life and Career (2020)

Gene Hackman: The Life and Work (2019)

Joanne Woodward: Her Life and Career (2019)

Philip Seymour Hoffman: The Life and Work (2017)

Anne Bancroft: The Life and Work (2017)

Neil Simon on Screen: Adaptations and Original Scripts for Film and Television (2015)

Gwen Verdon: A Life on Stage and Screen (2015)

Sandy Dennis: The Life and Films (2014)

Australian Horror Films, 1973–2010 (2012)

Frances Farmer: The Life and Films of a Troubled Star (2011)

Jules Dassin: The Life and Films (2011)

Grande Dame Guignol Cinema: A History of Hag Horror from Baby Jane *to* Mother (2009)

Mitzi Gaynor
Her Life and Career

PETER SHELLEY

McFarland & Company, Inc., Publishers
Jefferson, North Carolina

All photographs are from the author's collection.

Library of Congress Cataloguing-in-Publication Data

Names: Shelley, Peter, 1962– author.
Title: Mitzi Gaynor : her life and career / Peter Shelley.
Description: Jefferson, North Carolina : McFarland & Company, Inc., Publishers, 2024 | Includes bibliographical references and index.
Identifiers: LCCN 2024039725 | ISBN 9781476694528 (paperback : acid free paper) ∞
 ISBN 9781476694528 (ebook)
Subjects: LCSH: Gaynor, Mitzi, 1931– | Actresses—United States—Biography. | BISAC: BIOGRAPHY & AUTOBIOGRAPHY / Entertainment & Performing Arts | PERFORMING ARTS / Film / History & Criticism
Classification: LCC PN2287.G414 S54 2024 | DDC 792.02/8092 [B]—dc23/eng/20241010
LC record available at https://lccn.loc.gov/2024039725

British Library cataloguing data are available

ISBN (print) 978-1-4766-9452-8
ISBN (ebook) 978-1-4766-5374-7

© 2024 Peter Shelley. All rights reserved

No part of this book may be reproduced or transmitted in any form or by any means, electronic or mechanical, including photocopying or recording, or by any information storage and retrieval system, without permission in writing from the publisher.

Front cover image: Mitzi Gaynor from the 1957 film *Les Girls* (MGM/Photofest)

Printed in the United States of America

McFarland & Company, Inc., Publishers
 Box 611, Jefferson, North Carolina 28640
 www.mcfarlandpub.com

Table of Contents

Introduction 1

1. Beginning 7
2. 20th Century–Fox 21
3. *Jollyanna* 39
4. Marriage 54
5. *South Pacific* 73
6. Las Vegas 89
7. *Mitzi* 101
8. *Mitzi ... The First Time* 109
9. Life After Television 126
10. *Razzle Dazzle! My Life Behind the Sequins* 138
11. Death 149

Appendix of Work 151
Bibliography 155
Index 165

Introduction

In my constant search for new movie subjects to write about, I noticed Mitzi Gaynor. She had a brief filmography (which is always appealing) and relatively few television appearances. And unlike June Allyson, my last subject, she had not written a memoir. This was a surprise, particularly for a star of her era. I saw semi-recent interviews where Gaynor spoke about writing a book, but as of 2024, no book has been released. I learned that she was a published writer of articles and had written a foreword for Patty Farmer's 2017 book on the Plaza Hotel. Perhaps life intervened, as I also learned of her having health problems.

But sometimes a memoir does not give one the details one requires. June Allyson's book was a good example: The coverage of her career was spotty, though it did prove to be useful when I was writing my book on her. But I have written biographies without a memoir to help so I decided Gaynor's life and career were worth exploring. She had given a lot of public interviews but this was a double-edged sword, as her stories often had conflicting facts and names. But I hoped I could present a reasonably accurate chronology.

Gaynor's career has had an interesting trajectory from stage performer to movie star to nightclub performer to TV star and back to stage performer. She has reinvented herself multiple times to take advantage of opportunities and to change with the times.

I had only known Gaynor from *There's No Business Like Show Business* (1954) and I was only drawn to that film for Marilyn Monroe. I was aware Gaynor was in it but to me she was like Ethel Merman—someone I couldn't get excited about. I hadn't seen *South Pacific* (1958) or her television specials. So watching her movies from the start was an education.

Gaynor entered the movies after the great golden years in 1950,

Introduction

just as the studios were in crisis. The government had ordered the dismantling of movie theater chains, which had ensured distribution of each studio's product, and TV had captured the public's imagination. The studios were still signing up people to long-term contracts as Gaynor was signed but she would not last the seven years at 20th Century–Fox. They would give her supporting roles and then star her in leading roles in *Golden Girl* (1951) and *The I Don't Care Girl* (1953) but then she was back to supporting roles. This was perhaps because both *Golden Girl* and *The I Don't Care Girl* were flops. It then seemed Fox lost interest in her, even releasing Gaynor for three months so she could go back on stage for two months with the Civic Light Opera Association. The loss of interest was perhaps also due to Fox having another female contractee usurping all attention: Monroe.

Fox now had nothing for Gaynor so she played a supporting role in a Western by an independent company, which Fox distributed: *Three Young Texans* (1954). The studio gave her another supporting role in *There's No Business Like Show Business.* Among the cast was Monroe.

Gaynor was more talented than Monroe—a better singer, better dancer and better actress—but she lacked Monroe's erotic appeal. Gaynor was attractive in her own way—she had a dancer's body, a cute face and a chirpy persona. She was also not the problem that Monroe was. Her training on stage and personality made her a professional who was always on time and prepared. If performing was a struggle for Marilyn, it was not for Gaynor. But, despite her achievements, Mitzi was never the icon that Monroe became.

During production of *There's No Business Like Show Business,* Gaynor's Fox contract was terminated. Gaynor has alternately claimed that she wanted out and that Fox fired her. Ironically for *There's No Business Like Show Business,* Gaynor got some of her best notices. She even had to promote the film after she had left Fox, and on her honeymoon! But by this time, she had signed a new contract with Paramount. That four-picture deal only resulted in three films—a supporting role in *Anything Goes* (1956), the co-lead in *The Birds and the Bees* (1956) and a supporting role in *The Joker Is Wild* (1957).

Fox tried to get her back without success. She moved from Paramount to MGM for a supporting role in *Les Girls* (1957) before landing a much-coveted role in a film that was not produced by Fox but distributed by them. This was *South Pacific* (1958). The film was a box office success, but not the triumph for Gaynor that it should have been.

Introduction

Perhaps the role was haunted by its Broadway originator Mary Martin or by Doris Day, who people thought *should* have done it on film.

And then Gaynor never made another movie musical. Times had changed and, on the rare occasions that movie musicals were made, they were no longer the type that Gaynor fit into. She did make three comedies, even having the lead in *Happy Anniversary* (1959), but they were not successes. There were more offers but she decided to make another career change. Interestingly, Gaynor herself said that she was not good in movies, just ordinary. She didn't like the camera and felt the camera didn't like her. Maybe that was the difference between her and Monroe. The camera loved Marilyn.

A review of her film performances shows Gaynor was a good actress as well as a good dancer and singer. Watching the films in chronological order, one can see the development she made in acting ability, though this was also subject to the chances the role gave her. Musical comedy performers are undervalued in terms of the dramatic ability required in their straight scenes and Gaynor was a natural kind of performer from the start. When she advanced to more challenging parts, as in *The Joker Is Wild* which required a drunk scene and a scene where she rejects her fiancé, the actress was convincing.

Some felt that Gaynor did not have the chops to do the dramatic scenes in *South Pacific*—which included a difficult one where the character has to admit to racial prejudice. But those who feared she was not up to it had obviously not seen her earlier work. Gaynor also had a gift for being funny, including the ability to do accents, which was demonstrated in both her musicals and her later comedies. Among Gaynor's memorable movie moments, a favorite is her singing and dancing "The Johnson Rag" in *The I Don't Care Girl*. She is very amusing in *Happy Anniversary*, otherwise a heavy-handed film. She is perhaps best costumed in *Anything Goes* (1956), singing and dancing "It's De-lovely" with Donald O'Connor.

Gaynor achieved greater success post–Hollywood as a live performer. In Las Vegas from 1961 to 1972, she was said to have been a bigger draw than Frank Sinatra, and the deals she and her husband-manager Jack Bean brokered made her a wealthy woman. The act she created also gave her material that she could use in a series of eight television specials between 1968 and 1978. These specials give you an idea of what Gaynor was like as a live performer, as did her 1964 guest spot on *The Ed Sullivan Show*. On *Ed Sullivan*, Gaynor sang and danced "It's Too Darn Hot"

Introduction

and sang "The More I See You." Her TV specials are more problematic, marked by coverage of dance numbers that are undercut with medium camera shots. However, even with directorial missteps, the best numbers are the "Spinning Wheel" medley, a gypsy song and dance and "Those Were the Days" in *Mitzi's 2nd Special*.

Mitzi (1968), the first special, contains a segment featuring The Kid, which originated in her stage show. Gaynor, without makeup, plays a lonely little girl. The Kid returned for *Mitzi's 2nd Special* (1969) and *Mitzi ... The First Time* (1973). The deal for the TV specials, produced by a company created by Gaynor and Bean, added to her wealth.

She continued to perform in nightclubs and theaters. Gaynor in the 2000s created a one-woman show, *Razzle Dazzle! My Life Behind the Sequins*, in which she toured the United States and Canada until ill health slowed her down.

Her life was relatively free of scandal. The closest she came to infamy was in her relationship with Howard Hughes, who proposed to her. She was engaged to another man but technically still single. Gaynor closed the chapter on Hughes upon learning he had also proposed to a host of other ladies. After that she married Jack—a union that lasted for 54 years until his death in 2006. She did get hits from Baptist church elders for the burlesque strip tease in the stage musical *Jollyanna* in 1952, the Catholic Church for sweating on *The Ed Sullivan Show*, and others for allegedly refusing to lend the Beatles (who were also on the show) her hairdryer. Gaynor also had censor problems with two of her television specials: quoting "I don't give a damn" in a *Gone with the Wind* parody in *Mitzi's 2nd Special* and her "Lazy River" dance in *Mitzi ... What's Hot, What's Not* (1978). The former was allowed but the latter was subject to editing to obscure her nude-illusion costume.

What probably redeemed Gaynor was her sense of humor. If she played the diva or the sex goddess, it was with a wink. Gaynor said she was a Hungarian beef with a face like a pizza, whose brunette hair grew out blonde. So you knew this woman didn't take herself too seriously. In *Mitzi*, the Kid defaces portraits of Gaynor and then the real Gaynor appears wearing a glamorous gown and a fake moustache. On the same special, she plays a hillbilly who hopes to meet Mitzi Gaynor and comments on the star's bad-girl Bob Mackie costumes. In *Mitzi's 2nd Special*, the Kid parodies a photo of Gaynor in a glamorous pose.

She reported that her parents warned her about getting a big head in show business. Gaynor felt she never did. Gaynor was a professional

Introduction

and was grateful to her audiences. She loved the people who came to see her and those that showed an interest.

While this is the first book to span Gaynor's life and career, it cannot be considered the definitive study since some of the work is not available for viewing. I would love to see her first short *It's Your Health* (1949), made before she signed with Fox, and I was unable to see the entire *Kraft Music Hall* TV episode "Mitzi Gaynor Christmas Show." Also missed are her guest appearances on the Donald O'Connor television series *Here Comes Donald* (1954, 1955 and 1960) and Gaynor's singing on *The 31st Annual Academy Awards* (April 6, 1959), where she had to sing and re-sing the chorus of "There's No Business Like Show Business." I would also have liked to read Tony Charmoli's book *Stars in My Eyes*, since he directed five of Gaynor's TV specials. I also fear that my copy of her special *Mitzi and 100 Guys* (1975) is incomplete.

For the unavailable material as much information as possible has been provided. I have accessed online sources like the Internet Movie Database and Gaynor's own website and Facebook postings, as well as associated biographies and books on co-workers which allowed me to consider differing views of some of the events and situations. I also read articles and interviews that she gave to newspapers and magazines, accessing the archives of *The New York Times*, *Photoplay* magazine and eBay for photographs of Gaynor at events. The Getty Images website was also useful in this area. Additionally, eBay had stage show programs for me to look at and gather information from. I also found interviews on YouTube helpful.

The book is written as a biography, with Gaynor's career presented in the context of her life. Each film, TV, stage and radio show appearance is mixed into the biography. I have provided an analysis of the work when possible, positioning Gaynor's place in the project, commenting on her look and performance, and quoting any comments I have found by the star as well as those about her by director and co-stars. I have also given the critical reaction that the work received and information about any awards it earned. To complement the text, I have supplied stills, portraits, posters and lobby cards from some of her films and television shows. The book also comes with an appendix and a bibliography.

1

Beginning

Mitzi Gaynor was born in Chicago on September 4, 1931, as Francesca Frances Mitzi Marlene de Czanyi von Wise Gerber. Her parents were Henry de Czanyi von Gerber and his wife Pauline, *née* Fisher. Her astrological sign was Virgo and she was called "Baby Girl Gerber" on her birth certificate. Henry wanted to call her Irving and Pauline liked Anastasia, and they compromised on Mitzi.

Henry, a violinist, cellist, orchestra conductor and music director of Hungarian descent, came to the United States before World War I. He had been involved in the court of Franz Joseph but left Hungary with nothing but his cello. He conducted in theaters throughout America and Europe and for the opera singer Geraldine Farrar on a tour of South America. He gave up being a musician in 1930, so his daughter never knew him as one.

Pauline was a tall, blonde ballroom dancer and flapper from St. Louis with Viennese blood. A protégé of dancer Albertina Rush, Pauline looked like Marlene Dietrich. Gaynor said if you didn't comment on her resemblance to Dietrich, Pauline would. In Chicago, she had an act called Ernesto and Pauline at the Chez Paree nightclub and was famous for a dance called The Fish: She would run from the side of the stage and jump into the arms of Ernesto so she looked like a fish and then he would throw her up in the air. One time, Pauline flew into the lap of Al Capone in the audience. She decided to give up the business and have a baby. Pauline was also a very good shorthand typist.

Gaynor said that her mother was her greatest influence, admiring her vitality, quirkiness and good humor. Pauline loved parties and people, and these traits were passed down to her daughter. They had a great relationship. It was said that the mother hoped her daughter might achieve the stardom Pauline did not.

Their close bond contrasted sharply with the explosive dynamic between mother and father. The tempestuous, almost militant Henry had given up his career as a cellist to emigrate to America and struggled to find work during the Depression. Gaynor said that things were tough but not for her, since her parents would never let anything be tough for her. The family lived in Elgin, Illinois.

Pauline played music constantly and, at five months of age, her hazel-eyed brunette baby was waving her bottle and moving her feet and legs to the rhythm of records. Before the child could walk, she held onto a chair and bounced in time to the music. Mitzi could waltz at 18 months and at age three could do the polka and the gavotte (a French dance) and make deep curtseys. Gaynor attributed her talents to her parents.

The family moved to Detroit (which Gaynor would always jokingly pronounce "Detwa"). The girl would pick up the fallen leaves from the cherry tree in the yard behind theirs to make bouquets. The natural tomboy also climbed and picked the blossoms and cherries for her mother.

At four, Pauline and her sister Francine Woodbury reportedly took the girl to the ballet for the first time. There she was starry-eyed and sat more quietly than ever before in her life. Since the family didn't have much money, Pauline sat with her for the first act and Francine for the second. Then at home, Mitzi performed the first act for her aunt and the second act for her mother. While the girl danced, the women smoked cigarettes, drank sloe gin and read Tarot cards—and her father would tell her this was driving him crazy. Mitzi thought this was why she grew up with a skewed sense of humor.

Francine, a dancing teacher, tutored her niece in the basic ballet positions. Mitzi then graduated to learning the steps of Tchaikovsky's *Sleeping Beauty* suite. For ballet practice, the girl hung onto the bedpost. She loved every moment she was dancing. Pauline took her to see all the ballet shows that came to town, including the Ballet Russe. With Pauline and Francine, she cried at the loveliness of Markova, and learned to carry her head and hold her shoulders in the same way Markova did. Somehow the girl managed to secure a dollar's worth of a perfume called Ballerina. Her Markova personality lasted until the girl saw Claudette Colbert in a movie and decided to cut her hair in bangs and speak in the Colbert voice. The next one to be copied was Sonja Henie. Pauline made Mitzi little skating caps and mittens, and the girl twirled

1. Beginning

Portrait of the young ballerina Mitzi Gerber, later named Mitzi Gaynor.

and twisted on imaginary skates. When she saw the movie *Wuthering Heights* (1939), the girl sobbed uncontrollably and became terrified of falling in love. She declared that her whole life was to be given to dance.

Enrolled at the Tilden and Chandler Grade Schools, Mitzi was a good student, but she hated school: She wanted to do as well as she could and then get out as fast as possible to go to her dancing class. She said she never felt like a little girl. She never had birthday parties or had friends over, the latter perhaps because Mitzi always lived in apartments—and not in the best parts of town. Anything that she ever got or enjoyed pertained to the theater or movies. She and a girlfriend regularly took a bus to downtown Detroit on Saturday nights and went to the Fox Theatre to see Betty Grable movies. She would never forget those moments or that theater, which was a palace with beautiful statuary, artwork and tapestries. On Sundays, they wandered through the Art Institute, sitting on the cement benches inside and eating sandwiches. Mitzi saw her first television set at the Institute: It seemed like a wonderful alternative to listening to soap operas on the radio.

Boys annoyed her. They hung around and invited her to join their baseball team, which she agreed to do if they made her captain. Mitzi loved the feeling of the bat in her hands. After the games, she spread terror among the other girls when she swung freely. Mitzi swung at the boys too, particularly anyone who tried to cut in on her. When one boy tried to get her to buckle under, she dropped the bat and beat him up with her fists. One source claims that Mitzi became the captain of the baseball team.

At the age of eight, the girl contracted scarlet fever and spent 21 days at the Herman Keefer Hospital. Despite her illness, she had a ball. She loved the food and could have all the ice cream she wanted. The girl also loved the nurses who gave her manicures and Miss Deb toilet water, which she splashed all over an intern. When a nurse brought her hand lotion, Mitzi kissed his hands in gratitude. In no time she had the ward staff and patients doing boogie woogie. Mitzi learned the Latin names of the less familiar diseases and used them as swear words to scare the wits out of the less medically educated.

Out of hospital, she went back to dancing, every day working at the bar and strengthening her leg muscles. Mitzi may have not been a prima ballerina but she had a personality and energy that made her stand out. She later said being a ballerina was not for her because she couldn't keep her costume zipped up.

1. Beginning

The girl now felt ready for her public debut. On the big night, at the 11th hour, her usual accompanist fell ill and a substitute was provided. But Mitzi felt no stage fright. There was a quick rehearsal which went smoothly but, before the audience, the pianist went to bits. Mitzi's introductory number was supposed to be in 4–4 time but it sounded out in waltz rhythm as the girl whirled from the wings. Proving she had the stuff of stardom, Mitzi instantly became her own choreographer and changed the steps to fit the beat. The girl got through the performance triumphantly, and this led to appearances at women's clubs. She said that doing "In a Persian Market" in an Oriental costume with a pianist, for four ladies having luncheon in a tea room, was quite a sight. The self-described brat wore her first bra and high heels at age ten.

Her next dancing teacher was the exacting ballet mistress Madame Kathryn Etienne at the Silver Studios. Of French-Greek heritage, Etienne had danced all over Europe in her day. Madame didn't believe in little girls going to ballet class because it ruined their legs, but she agreed to take Mitzi on, and became the first teacher to allow the girl to express her natural sense of comedy in the dance. Having seen Carmen Miranda in the stage musical revue *The Streets of Paris*, Mitzi imitated her. Madame adored it, especially when the girl swung to boogie woogie. Mitzi adored her back, feeling that Madame really understood her. She always remembered Madame telling her to dance from the heart and to *give*.

Madame predicted that Mitzi would go to Hollywood and become a big movie star. Madame's brother Nico was married to Cyd Charisse, and Madame thought the connection would benefit her star pupil. So when Mitzi was 11, Pauline decided to make the move to California. Madame felt it was *her* time to go as well. Mitzi's father was against his daughter being in show business, and this meant she would see little of him in the future. Mitzi, Pauline and Francine took the train to Los Angeles confident that Mitzi would become a star. The ambitious Pauline would help her daughter use her brains and body in the desire to succeed. They were to discover, like so many thousands before them, the difference between smart commercial professionalism and dreamy-eyed amateurism.

When they arrived in Los Angeles, they didn't have a dime. Pauline took a series of jobs that allowed her to be with her daughter as much as possible and to cover the cost of lessons and costumes. The latter needed repeated replacing as the girl's height shot up. Enrolled at Le Conte

Junior High, she learned that on Monday mornings, the girls bleached their hair in the lavatory, dried it in the sun and appeared in class with bleached stripes. This look was later called the California Stripes.

Mitzi joined the Powers Professional School, run by the mother of future actress Mala Powers. By now she was too old to be a child star and too young to be a teenager. At the Powers School, everyone was just as ambitious as Mitzi was. But this spurred the girl's sense of competition. She learned as much there in half a day as she had learned in public school in a week.

Mitzi's exposure to stars was fleeting. One day she walked by actor Herbert Marshall in the street as he was being photographed. The girl bought all the newspapers for weeks hoping to see herself in the published photograph, but it never appeared. In a department store, she saw Lena Horne and bought all of her records.

Mitzi's vow to live for dance and not for love changed when she discovered that boys could be more than a nuisance. There were several candidates at the Powers School but the girl was particularly taken with the high school boy who had been voted best all-around athlete. She could see that high school boys scared easily so a girl had to play it cool. But Mitzi was not subtle expressing her crush, her mouth falling open every time she saw him. The girl was never late for class when he was in it, for fear of missing him. Mitzi studied hard so that she could show off and was always finding excuses to stroll past the football field. Mitzi persuaded a friend to give a birthday party so she could have the boy go with her, but ballet class got in the way. On *his* birthday, his mother gave a party and Mitzi was invited. But the hoped-for romance never happened, and as this was wartime, he was soon drafted.

Another boy succeeded him in her heart, giving Mitzi his frat pin. When she had the opportunity to go to New York for a show, he didn't want her to go, but she did, and wore his pin. In New York, Mitzi and Pauline bunked at the Hotel Edison where, because of the war shortage, nobody was allowed to stay more than five days. But the hotel clerk found the girl so enchanting that he let them stay for two weeks. To avoid being found out, they dared not raise their blinds.

Mitzi had engagements with the corps of the Ballet Russe when it appeared in Los Angeles. For *Coppelia*, Mitzi was paid $2 by Anton Dolan. During the performance, she fell onto the stage from a camouflaged scaffold. The girl had been so engrossed in her interpretation that she enthusiastically danced off the edge and into the air.

1. Beginning

Her salary increased to $4 when she gave a formal recital on July 7, 1944, in the Redlands Bowl in California with other members of the Etienne Ballet. Mitzi continued to study with Madame Etienne: ballet, tap, modern and interpretive dance. Cyd Charisse came to the school and danced a little for them. The girl had never seen anybody so beautiful. Charisse was kind to her, and the two remained friends. Mitzi was still performing for Madame's dance group at the age of 13, earning $5.

Dancing in USO shows for soldiers, Mitzi did imitations of Carmen Miranda, Danny Kaye and Russian ballet stars. The girl was the featured comedienne-dancer of the Air Force Hollywood Variety Show. For six months, they traveled by airplane to all the bases in 40 states between Los Angeles and Charleston, South Carolina. She studied with Aida Bronbadt aka Broadbent, who placed her in the New Year's Eve festival at the Pasadena Playhouse and paid her $15.

On October 6, the girl appeared at the Wilshire Ebell Theatre as Annabel Stuart in the musical comedy *Home on the Range*, singing "Hollywood" by Aubrey Stauffer.

Mitzi lied about her age, saying she was three years older, and in

Mitzi (top center) in Kathryn Etienne's Dance Troupe.

San Francisco got a job as a dancer in *Song Without Words: The Life and Times of Peter Ilyich Tchaikovsky*. This was produced by James Dolittle and directed by Aida Bronbadt, with Anton Dolan as choreographer. Mitzi told an alternate story where her mother worked for Dolittle and asked if Mitzi could audition for the show. The girl met Dolan, who was going to work at Madame's school. Mitzi also told how Madame had brought Dolan to see her, but he was unimpressed by the girl's attitude. Nevertheless, she got in the show's ballet, which paid $65 a week. In addition, she had one line, "Flowers for the lady," which she got to say three times. The plan was for the show to go to New York after its Los Angeles engagement, but Mitzi and Pauline decided she should not go with it. But then the show closed out of town anyway.

As Aida Bronbadt was now dance director of the Civic Light Opera Association in Los Angeles, Mitzi asked her for a job. Los Angeles had not been considered a great theater town until the Association staged Broadway-quality productions that sometimes had additional runs in San Francisco and Philadelphia. The company's manager Edwin Lester said that when he saw Mitzi, her talent was obvious and he was intent on making her a star. In 1946, the 14-year-old danced a comedy bit in her first Association show, *Roberta*. The show was well-received. A few weeks later, Mitzi was assigned to their next production, *The Gypsy Lady*, a wedding of two Victor Herbert operettas (*The Fortune Teller* and *Serenade*). The girl reportedly played a dancing gypsy. One source has her appearing in *The Fortune Teller* in California and the composite *Gypsy Lady* when it went to New York. At the New Century Theatre, it ran for 72 or 79 performances from September 1946.

Mitzi came to New York with Pauline for the show. Edwin Lester was so impressed with Mitzi that he had her join the Association's tour of *Song of Norway*, a show about composer Edvard Grieg, in Philadelphia in 1947. Again Pauline traveled with her daughter. One source claims Mitzi played the part of Miss Anders, singing and dancing "Bon Vivant Part 2" with comedian Sig Arno. Mitzi had been sent as a cast replacement and was said to have gone on after only three rehearsals. She got pushed onstage at the right time and was beckoned off for the exits. Mitzi would say that Arno was helpful and encouraging. He reportedly came offstage on opening night and told the girl the applause was all for her. Another source says that he also pushed her out again on stage to take the bows alone. Mitzi hoped

1. Beginning

that, if she ever became a star, she would be as kind to a newcomer as Arno was to her.

Another source claims that Miss Anders was simply a speaking part. In his book *Unsung Genius: The Passion of Dancer Choreographer Jack Cole*, Glenn Loney quotes composer Robert Wright and his writing partner George "Chet" Forrest, who say that Mitzi was only one of a flock of children.

The show moved to Chicago for 16 weeks; opened at the Los Angeles Philharmonic Auditorium, and ended in San Francisco. Next came the Association's production of Irving Berlin's *Louisiana Purchase*. The girl was cast as Emmy Lou, who was featured in the reprise of the title song, and sang and danced "You Can't Brush Me Off" with Tommy Rall. Berlin came to the last week of rehearsal and introducing himself to Mitzi as she waited in the wings for her entrance. She chewed gum during their chat and he liked her moxie. Gaynor said they stayed in touch, and that she sent him a telegram on his birthday every year.

In 1948's *Naughty Marietta*, she played Claudet, who sang "Personality" and "I've Been Looking for the Perfect Man" and was in the title number. *The Great Waltz* followed in 1949. Edwin Lester saw the girl clowning backstage, impersonating an aging ballerina and a nervous beginner. He decided to write a comic role for her with Aida Bronbadt devising a comic ballet. Sources differ as to which show this was for, but the number was said to be the highlight. In *The Great Waltz*, she played Katie, the Toast of Vienna, and danced the comic ballet with George Zoritch of the Ballet Russe.

Mitzi later reported that while doing *The Great Waltz*, she went to MGM to get a job that they ultimately decided that Mitzi was too young for: "the other woman" in the musical comedy *The Barkleys of Broadway* (1949). When she passed Gene Kelly on the lot, he said, "Well, aren't you going to say hello, Miss Gerber?" and then he proceeded to sing a verse from one of her numbers from *The Great Waltz*, which he had seen a couple days before.

The Great Waltz transferred to the Curran Theatre in San Francisco, opening in April 1949. The girl sang "Buzza Buzza Buzza," "The State of the Dance" and "Radetzky." In one San Francisco performance, she lost her petticoat while dancing with Walter Slezak. Mitzi knew it was slipping and she was in agony. Slezak tried to propel her to the wings but the falling petticoat handicapped him. The girl nonchalantly slipped out of it and whirled to center stage, blushing. The audience reportedly loved her for it and their applause drowned out the music when she took her bow. Another version has the girl high-kicking the fallen petticoat into the wings and singing her way back to center stage.

Mitzi described herself as a "triple threat" who knew classical music and could sing and dance and play comedy. She was exuberant and openly flirted with Edwin Lester in front of the entire company, patting his behind or plopping herself in the man's lap. Everyone thought Mitzi had him in the palm of her hand. She also studied the veteran performers around her, learning every entertainment trick in the book. She was especially quick to learn the art of telling a story to help her connect with an audience.

Mitzi also learned not to be quite a snot, after one day throwing her shoes and dance case on the floor and stomping out of rehearsal. Another dancer, an older girl, found Mitzi in the lavatory. When Mitzi refused to come out of the stall, the woman reached inside, grabbed her foot and dragged her out kicking and screaming. She was told if this behavior continued, ground glass would be put in her toe shoes-- and the girl believed it. Then the older dancer offered her a cigarette.

The company was a close-knit group which had been together for more than three years. While they claimed to depend on each other, they could be mean to Mitzi. They upstaged her in the few little scenes she had, walked in on song cues, and killed the laughs. But without these humbling experiences, Mitzi might have become a conceited monster. Here she was given the luckiest break of her life and the real troopers shrunk Mitzi's head back to its normal size. They showed her how little she knew and how much she had to learn about the business. She had this treatment coming to her and Mitzi was forever grateful for it.

Doing one show in San Francisco, Mitzi went on her first date: A theater usher named Fred took her to have black-and-white sodas and grilled cheese sandwiches.

Mitzi carried on with her ballet dance classes, going to various teachers. She believed that you got something new and different from each teacher. You eventually blended all their various methods into something that became known as your own particular style.

Mitzi and her mother rented a furnished three-storey house overlooking the Hollywood Hills. After winning herself a small army of would-be beaus, new love came with the distinguished, prematurely

1. Beginning

gray-haired Los Angeles attorney Richard Brown Coyle. Thirteen years her senior, he had gone backstage to visit Edward Everett Horton in *Naughty Marietta*. For Mitzi, it was love at first sight: He was the most beautiful thing she had ever seen, male or female, and the perfect candidate to lose her virginity to. To arrange an introduction, the girl bumped into him with a box of candy and offered him some. She and Richard became engaged after only a month. Mitzi knew it was right to marry someone outside her own profession; and attorneys were logical and unemotional. He was a calming influence (which she needed). Because they met on a Thursday, they had a date every Thursday night.

In 1949, Mitzi appeared in the 18-minute short *It's Your Health* for the Southern Californian Dental Association. She played Peggy Hendricks, the girlfriend of star halfback Jim Davis (Johnny Sands), who has failed his Annapolis dental examination.

By the time of *The Great Waltz*, Edwin Lester wanted Mitzi to do well as she was under contract to him for a reported $135 a week. The better the girl did, the more money he would make. She chose an agent whose card was engraved in gold, because to her that meant more money. His only client was Hopalong Cassidy.

There are three versions of how Mitzi went from stage productions to the films of 20th Century–Fox. The first is that an assistant to George Jessel saw her and told his boss about it. Jessel was looking for a girl to play Lotta Crabtree in his pet project *Golden Girl*. This led to Jessel going to see Mitzi in *The Great Waltz*.

The second version has Jessel in the audience that witnessed the fallen petticoat incident. He said that two minutes after seeing Mitzi on stage, he knew she was the greatest young personality in show business and that he had his Lotta. She sparkled like champagne. danced liked a dream, sang like a lark, and made him laugh and cry. Jessel felt the girl would be the next big star in Hollywood.

The third version had an assistant to Fox producer Sol C. Siegel and director Henry Koster see *The Great Waltz*. They were looking for a girl to play a supporting role in the new Betty Grable Fox musical *My Blue Heaven*.

Mitzi said her performance in *The Great Waltz* was noticed by composer Cole Porter and Koster. But all this attention was because of magic slippers, her lucky purple-toed shoes that she wore on the first day of the shooting of every film. Jack Bean reported that the press coverage of her fallen petticoat really got her noticed. Koster says in

Richard Brown Coyle and Gaynor re-enacted their meeting at the Philharmonic Auditorium where she appeared in the Los Angeles Civic Light Opera Association production of *Naughty Marietta* in 1948.

1. Beginning

Irene Kahn Atkins' book *Henry Koster: A Directors Guild of America Oral History* how charming Mitzi was on stage and that he wanted her to make a screen test. She reported that when they met, Koster pinched her cheek and Mitzi told him to take his hands off her. Koster told her he was a famous director but she didn't care—she still didn't want him to touch her. She was trying to be funny and luckily the man did not take offense.

Edwin Lester wanted her to audition for Cole Porter's new show *Out of This World*, a musical adaptation of Jean Giraudoux's play *Amphitryon 38*. Lester arranged for her to go to Porter's house in Beverly Hills. He gave Mitzi money to buy a nice dress and shoes to replace the dirndl skirts and blouses and huarache shoes she wore, plus some jewelry. Mitzi went to the Broadway Department Store and brought a Mexican broomstick skirt for $1.50, a white Mexican off-the-shoulder blouse for $1 and twisted silver earrings for 50 cents or $1. She took the bus out to Beverly Hills wearing her normal clothes, not wanting to mess up the new outfit. Off the bus, Mitzi changed in a gas station or drug store and then took a taxi to Porter's house on Hummingbird Lane.

She had never seen Porter so when a man came to the door, the girl assumed it was him. It was the butler, and he took her to the lanai. She explored, lifting up the cushions on a sofa, looking at photographs and eating the candy. When Mitzi turned around, she saw that Porter was seated at the piano, observing. Mitzi wanted to sing a Porter song but when Porter told her he couldn't play it, she responded, "Well, you wrote it, didn't you?!" So instead the girl sang *a cappella*—and got the job. Another version of the story has her asking to sing "Anything Goes" but at a slower tempo; he replied that the song didn't go in a slower tempo. But Mitzi told him to try it. So he did and she sang and danced around. Porter commented on her energy and she replied it was pep, mouthing off to the great man. Playing the soubrette opposite David Wayne would pay $250 a week.

The girl's screen test for Fox was arranged by Henry Koster, Sol C. Siegel and George Jessel. She had a three-way screen test—singing, dancing and acting—shot both in black-and-white and color. Mitzi said it was a hoot. The funniest thing about was her makeup. They spent the whole morning on it and she was hoping to end up looking like Joan Crawford, Lana Turner or Ava Gardner. But when the makeup man stepped aside and let her look in the mirror, the girl was crushed. She looked just like herself.

Mitzi sang "I'm in Love with a Wonderful Guy" from the stage musical *South Pacific*, years before she sang it in the film version. Then she was asked to dance a little ballet number on a black glass floor. She attached a piece of rubber to the tip of her shoes to keep her from slipping but, when she made her entrance, the rubber caught on the floor and she fell flat on her ass. The girl had never been in front of a microphone and spoke very loudly, projecting as if in the theater.

She was told the test was a success but then heard nothing from Fox. Finally Koster and Siegel called her in to talk about *My Blue Heaven*. They offered to sign the girl for $85 a week but she was making $125 a week in *The Great Waltz*. They were stunned that Mitzi turned down their offer. Presumably they saw their error, and a second offer ($1000 a week) led her to choose doing the film over the Cole Porter show. This was also a wise choice since the stage show did not start until November 1950. But Mitzi also wanted to be a movie star, or what she called a *boobie* star. This was because girls who were well-endowed (as she was) were already stars.

2

20th Century–Fox

One source claims that Mitzi was signed to a one-film deal but others assert that it was a seven-year contract. Jessel planned to star her in *Golden Girl* after Mitzi had done warm-ups in smaller roles. But first he suggested a name change. Mitzi was okay but Gerber sounded like a delicatessen. Jessel asked if Gaynor was Jewish. No, Catholic. Was she from the Gerber baby food company? No. He said Gerber was not an attractive name for a movie star and she was furious. He suggested Gaynor, after Janet Gaynor, who had made millions for Fox 20 years prior. Janet Gaynor also happened to be an actress that Mitzi's father loved. This was acceptable to Mitzi, partly because she didn't have to change the initials on the two beautiful handmade white leather suitcases her father had given her. Her name was reportedly officially changed in May 1950. The new Gaynor got a laugh from a cab driver who picked her up one morning to take her to the studio. He told her, "I have been an admirer of yours since I saw you in *7th Heaven*" (a 1927 silent movie with Janet Gaynor).

The Fox people were concerned because she wasn't a blonde. Gaynor said they could blonde her hair, so they lightened the color but it didn't work. She recalled her delayed meeting with production boss Darryl F. Zanuck as one of low comedy instead of deep drama. Mitzi was leaving the lot, comfortably gowned in a faded wash dress and old scruffs on her feet after a dance class, when the call came to go to Zanuck's office. Mitzi gave two accounts of what transpired. One version had her meet Zanuck, who told her that she looked terrible and looked much better on screen before dismissing her from his office. The second version has her waiting for him, sitting in a chair and attempting to hide her scruffs in the rug to present a well-poised appearance. She then found herself looking up into his amused eyes.

Zanuck asked her age and if she was married, and Gaynor answered ("18" and "No"). Then, with the meeting over, she exited by scuffling her feet along, all the way back across the room to the door. But Gaynor said she was not scared of Zanuck because he came from Hungarian stock like her.

In his book on Betty Grable, *The Girl with the Million Dollar Legs*, Tom McGee wrote that Gaynor was the third musical star at Fox, after Grable and June Haver. Zanuck kept her waiting on the sidelines, not wanting to entrust a virtually untried newcomer with a big-budget production. She was a talented dancer but Zanuck put her under the tutelage of a drama coach while he searched for a suitable role for her. This is in opposition to the idea that Gaynor had been hired specifically for a role in Fox's *My Blue Heaven*. She was happy to be given Betty Grable's makeup man and was taught grooming and hair styling. Mitzi also underwent rigid dieting and plenty of exercise for her transformation into a screen star.

The Technicolor musical *My Blue Heaven* (1950) was produced by Sol C. Siegel and directed by Koster with the working title *Storks Don't Bring Babies*. It was shot at Fox from December 5, 1949, to January 10, 1950, with an additional musical sequence shot later.. The screenplay was by Lamar Trotti and Claude Binyon, based on a story by S.K. Lauren. It's set in New York, where Kitty Moran (Grable) and her husband Jack (Dan Dailey), a song-and-dance team, want to adopt children. Gaynor, fifth-billed, plays the supporting role of Gloria Adams. We have to wait 30 minutes to see her on a television monitor singing and dancing the TV commercial parody "Cosmo Cosmetics" (music by Harold Arlen and lyrics by Ralph Blane). Gaynor is funny in the number, using a comic refined accent and dancing on her toes. She is also seen dancing with the TV show's dance director (the film's dance director Billy Daniel) and Jack in a rehearsal for "My Blue Heaven" (music by Walter Donaldson, lyrics by George Whiting).

Gloria as a better dancer than Kitty becomes a plot point when Gloria replaces Kitty on a show because Kitty has to stay home to look after her baby. The song-and-dance number with Gloria and Jack is "Live Hard, Work Hard, Love Hard" (by Arlen and Blane). Mitzi has a brunette hair extension by uncredited stylist Marie Bresselle. When we see Kitty watching the number on TV, she does some of the same sensual moves that Gloria dances, though not the balletic ones, probably because Kitty is wearing a long, tight skirt. Gloria as Kitty's replacement continues when Kitty decides to temporarily retire from the show to be a mother. Gloria isn't quite the Other Woman in the plot since while Jack kisses her, he really isn't interested in her. Additionally, her supposed love of Jack is a sign of career ambition but leavened by Gaynor's youth, likability and humor. Gloria's confession to Kitty that she is in love with Jack is offset by Kitty's calm and Jack's comic hysterical defensiveness. The problem is resolved easily with a threat that Kitty could have her fired.

Gaynor is funny flirting with Jack. She is also chased, forcibly made to drink by Walter Pringle (David Wayne) at a party, has her nose pulled by Jack and also kisses Jack. When Gloria reprises the Cosmo Cosmetics song to introduce Kitty and Jack doing "The Friendly Islands," she wears a white dress by costume director Charles LeMaire that has a sheer low-cut top and silver jewels that underline her breasts.

The film was released on September 15, 1950. It was praised by Aubrey Solomon and Tony Thomas in *The Films of 20th Century–Fox.*

(From left) Dan Dailey, Betty Grable and Mitzi in a lobby card for *My Blue Heaven* (1950).

According to *Variety*, Gaynor was the real eye-catcher of the pic. Bosley Crowther of *The New York Times* said she danced colorfully and sang nicely. The film was a box office success. When it was adapted for the airwaves (*Lux Radio Theater*) on February 25, 1952, Gaynor was not in the cast.

During her first day on the set, Mitzi didn't know what a mark was, so when she had to say her first line to Grable, she just walked over it and started talking. She cast a shadow over Grable, and the sound man threw off his earphones because of Mitzi's theatrical projecting. They tried again and three more times she missed the mark. A 2×4 was finally put on the floor for her but the girl tripped over it. Dan Dailey took her aside and told her to relax. He said this was not an opening night; she said it *was*, to her! Dailey and Grable were happy she was in the film and they both loved her. Gaynor later said that it was quite a way to start out in movies, with those wonderful people being so kind to her.

Gaynor apologized to Grable about the shadow and Grable confided that she had done the same thing when first co-starring with Alice Faye. But Gaynor was so fan-struck over Grable that she followed her around, even into the rest room. Gaynor would look under the stall and ask if she was all right. Grable finally ordered, "Get that kid away from me," but they soon became friends. Mitzi was impressed with Grable's no-nonsense approach to work. Grable also took the trouble to point out many technical details and helped Mitzi in every way possible. The raw newcomer to films felt Grable was very generous to her. It was said that Gaynor won over cast and crew with her playfulness, enthusiastic personality and a surprisingly innocent sweetness.

Grable was the bread-and-butter star of the studio; without her, everyone else would have been out of work. What made Gaynor mad was the suggestion that she was being groomed to take Grable's place. It was no secret that Grable was lately more interested in her home, family and friends than making movies. But the idea that Gaynor could be the new Grable was ridiculous. No one could be that; Grable was in a class by herself.

Henry Koster reported that he had much fun on the set with Gaynor, a beautifully built young lady and a good dancer and performer. After *My Blue Heaven*, the director didn't see her for a long time though Gaynor sent him Christmas cards.

Larry Billman in *Betty Grable: A Bio-Bibliography* wrote that

2. 20th Century–Fox

Grable's legendary comment to Marilyn Monroe ("Honey, I've had it. Go get yours. It's your turn now") was also said to Gaynor. Billman theorized that perhaps Grable said it to every newcomer she worked with. Tom McGee claimed in his Grable book that Grable strongly suspected that Gaynor *was* being groomed to replace her but didn't begrudge the youngster the chance. She found Gaynor to be a charming girl, never acting pushy or trying to upstage anyone. Grable helped Gaynor with her scenes and insisted that she be given the "Live Hard, Work Hard, Love Hard" number because it contained too many ballet steps. Grable was quoted in the July 1952 *Photoplay* as saying that Gaynor was better suited for the number because Grable had not done ballet in a long time. Grable was also glad to be out of the number because she felt she had enough dancing to do in the film. McGee also wrote that Grable was unnerved by Gaynor always being around when the older star did her production numbers. Grable reportedly commented to Dailey that Gaynor watched her every move and it was as if she was being understudied. McGee implied that after the shoot, Zanuck promoted Gaynor to her first starring role in the Fox musical *Golden Girl* though that film did not actually start production until April 30, 1951.

In his book *Betty Grable: The Reluctant Movie Star*, Doug Warren wrote that there was no conflict between Grable and Gaynor, with Fox's musical queen welcoming the aspiring starlet with warmth and cordiality. Grable even went to Zanuck to applaud her co-star, thinking she was great and worthy of more important tasks than those assigned to her in the film. Grable suggested that Gaynor be given a production number of her own and Zanuck saw to it that her part was expanded.

Grable also reportedly spent many hours with Gaynor, teaching her professional secrets. When *Saturday Evening Post* photographer Gene Lester visited the set, he found the two women huddled together with Grable coaching Gaynor on her role.

Doug Warren wrote that although Grable and Dailey made the film a hit, it was Gaynor who garnered the most studio publicity. She did not achieve stardom at this time but it was not for want of Zanuck trying. She had taken her first steps toward stardom and was rewarded with a salary increase.

After ballerina Valerie Bettis was tested for the role, it was announced in June 1950 that Gaynor would star in producer George Jessel's *The Belle of Market Street*, based on the life of Lotta Crabtree.

However, she made another film first. Director Jean Negulesco's drama *Take Care of My Little Girl* (1951) was shot at Fox from October 14 to mid–November. The screenplay was by Julius J. and Philip G. Epstein, based on the novel by Peggy Goodin. Jeanne Crain starred as Midwestern College student Liz Erickson, who learns some hard truths about sorority life, including snobbery and the cruelty of hazing. Gaynor, third-billed, plays the supporting role of Liz's roommate, Tucson-born Adelaide Swanson. Eighteen-year-old Adelaide has a good entrance, exiting a train with a quip to a short baggage man: "Are you kidding? Hey, wait a minute. I'll carry you." Gaynor gets to dance with two boys in a party scene, but in a conventional way because the film is not a musical. Her character has no real impact on the plot after Liz moves into the sorority house and juggles two love interests. Adelaide's wardrobe (by costumer Travilla) gets unique primary colors with a red blouse and blue skirt, when everyone else is dressed in pastels.

Her brash character has a loud speaking voice and, for the little she has to do, the actress is funny with eyebrow-raising at the sorority singing traditions. Her easy style contrasts with Crain, who was six years older and her acting less natural. It's also interesting how Carol Brannon as fellow student Casey Krausse has a ballpark resemblance to Gaynor though Bannon's brunette hair has bleached bangs. The two get a scene together where they banter but Carol has a more sizable role in the plot.

Released on July 6, 1951, the film was a box office success. It was praised by *Variety* and Bosley Crowther in *The New York Times*, the latter writing that Gaynor was original and amusing. A radio version of the film was broadcast on *Lux Radio Theater* on February 4, 1952, though without Gaynor. It was remade as the Italian-French romantic comedy *Fanciulle di lusso* aka *Luxury Girls* (1952).

It was reported that Gaynor called Jean Peters who plays student Dallas Prewitt "Pete" and Jeanne Crain "Dreamface." The actresses were said to have become her best friends on the Fox lot.

On October 31 came the announcement that Gaynor would appear in the Fox musical *Friendly Island*, to be directed by Edmund Goulding. On December 28, it was reported that Gaynor had taken over the role previously scheduled for Debra Paget and that the film would begin production on January 29, 1951.

Friendly Island was renamed *Down Among the Sheltering Palms* (1952). It was shot at Fox from February 19 to mid–March with additional scenes shot in April and October. The screenplay by Claude Binyon, Albert Lewin and Burt Styler (based on a story by Edward Hope) focused on Army Captain W.W. "Bill" Willoby (William Lundigan), head of the occupation force on Midi Island in the South Pacific, where it is forbidden to fraternize with the inhabitants. Third-billed Gaynor plays the supporting role of native princess Rozouila, who is given to Bill as a gift by the native King Jilouili (Billy Gilbert). She wears a long brunette wig and tropical makeup and speaks with an accent.

Rozouila appears in two musical numbers, "The Drum Chant" (by Ken Darby) and "What Makes De Diff'rence" (music by Harold Arlen and lyrics by Ralph Bane). In the former, Gaynor is unwrapped from a white cape to be revealed in a light brown patterned sarong with a split leg and a bone necklace, with flowers in her hair. She dances in front of eight native drummers, sometimes brandishing a long drumstick and jumping on top of the drums. The dance was staged by Seymour Felix. Her second number has Gaynor in the same Travilla-designed outfit *sans* bone necklace and she sings with her accent. Rozouila hangs around in the jungle near the hut where Bill has placed her since he doesn't want the girl living with him. This number shows the actress as vulnerable as opposed to the manic energy she brought to the dance. Gaynor sings two reprises of the song.

Rozouila gets two more patterned Travilla sarongs but with bare midriffs. The role also has her throw a coconut at Angela Toland (Gloria DeHaven) and Bill, and hide under an overturned crate. Gaynor gives a broad, funny performance when Rozouila describes how she will be punished if sent back to the king, and how the hut has an evil spirit. She also comically flutters her eyelashes at Colonel Thomas B. Richards (the uncredited Fay Roope).

The film's release was delayed until March 1, 1953. Its taglines included "It's That Maiden-Mad, G.I.-Glad Tropical Musical Jamboree." It was a box office disappointment. It was praised by Tony Thomas and Aubrey Solomon in *The Films of 20th Century–Fox*. Howard H. Thompson of *The New York Times* wrote that Gaynor stopped the show cold, or hot, as usual.

This was one of three films that Gaynor made simultaneously, the others being *Golden Girl* and *The I Don't Care Girl*. Gaynor loved being so busy and said there was lots of hair dye changes between the three. She would have dark hair at eight a.m. and auburn by three p.m.

Lobby card for *Down Among the Sheltering Palms* (1952).

Producer George Jessel's *Belle of Market Street* was now renamed *Golden Girl*. The shooting of the musical Western was delayed for three weeks after Gaynor suffered a broken toe. With Lloyd Bacon as director, the film began production on location in San Francisco but was otherwise shot at Fox from April 30 to July 31. It was reported on May 9 that production was shut down temporarily when Gaynor lost her voice from laryngitis. The screenplay was by Walter Bullock, Charles O'Neal and Gladys Lehman from a story by Albert Lewis, Arthur Lewis and Edward Thompson. Gaynor starred as song-and-dance artiste Lola Crabtree, first seen as a 16-year-old working her way across America during the Civil War. She is first heard singing "Oh, Dem Golden Slippers" (by James Allen Bland) with her back to the camera as she plays an organ.

She performs several other numbers: "California Moon" (music by Joe Cooper and lyrics by George Jessel and Sam Lerner); "Kiss Me Quick and Go" (music by Frederick Buckley and lyrics by Silas Sexton Steel, sung with Dennis Day and Lotta's Band Members), "Sunday Morning" (music by Ken Darby and lyrics by Darby and Eliot Daniel, sung and danced with Day), "Carry Me Back to Old Virginny" (also by Bland, sung

2. 20th Century–Fox

with Day), a reprise of "Kiss Me Quick and Go" where Gaynor sings with the Band Members and dances, a reprise of "California Moon" where she sings and dances with James Barton, "When Johnny Comes Marching Home" (by Louis Lambert, singing and dancing with chorus boys) and "(I Wish I Was in) Dixie's Land" (by Daniel Decatur Emmett, sung with Day). Gaynor is perhaps best showcased in "When Johnny Comes Marching Home" where she appears to wear tropical makeup, and changes from a white knee-length dress to a black leotard with tutu.

The role also has Gaynor speaking in a French accent, crying, and swapping kisses with Tom Richmond (Dale Robertson). She makes Lotta likable and funny, especially wearing a fake beard mocking Mart Taylor (Dennis Day), and mimicking Tom's Southern accent. Despite Lola's youth, she has some emotionally adult moments. Lola is seen in her underwear, some low-cut dresses and in the abovementioned tutu. The dances are staged by Seymour Felix. Director Bacon gives Gaynor her first film closeups.

Golden Girl, released on November 1, was not a box office success. *The New York Times*' Bosley Crowther wrote that Gaynor was youthful and fresh. The song "Never" (music by Lionel Newman, lyrics by Eliot Daniel, sung by Dennis Day) received an Academy Award nomination.

Gaynor said that as a girl she read a book about Lotta Crabtree. Gaynor and director Bacon became very good friends after an initial awkwardness where he did not know what do with her. Gaynor had the feeling she had been given to him as a punishment. But she called him "Admiral" and saluted him, as he had been an admiral in the navy. Gaynor reported being told stories about Florenz Ziegfeld by James Barton and Seymour Felix, who both worked with him. Gaynor felt that Felix liked and understood her.

While in dance rehearsals, Gaynor broke a little toe and ended up with a cast up to the knee. With the production start date approaching, she started praying to St. Jude and in no time doctors removed the cast. Gaynor began to walk again and was able to dance without the slightest discomfort. This incident gave her faith in the saints.

Dale Robertson commented that she had more talent than anyone else at Fox, with the possible exception of Betty Grable. To Robertson, Gaynor always seemed happy, whether on or off-camera.

In an interview, Gaynor said that her love of ballet was shown by collecting pictures and books about Anna Pavlova. She loved clothes, especially shoes, and bought as many as her budget would permit. Her favorite possession was her 1946 car; at home, she answered to the nickname Tootie; her biggest dislike was affected people. One of Gaynor's rules of living was "Always be yourself." She loved music, good conversation and originality of thought and expression.

While in San Francisco promoting the film, Gaynor was visited backstage by Mrs. Mack, a past tutor. Mack said she had despaired of the girl's arithmetic back then but now had no need to worry. After seeing her on screen, Mack knew Gaynor would always be able to pay people to add and subtract for her.

Over the next several months, Fox didn't miss a chance to promote their latest ingenue, keeping her in the public eye. On June 20, it was announced that they had purchased a property by Phoebe and Henry Ephron entitled "The Girl Who Couldn't Help It," a musical about physical culture, as a vehicle for Gaynor. The film would be later produced by Robert Bassler, with the Ephrons writing the screenplay. On June 26, it was reported that she would play the top role of Judy Abbott in *Daddy Long Legs*, the romantic story of an orphan girl; it had been filmed twice since it was produced as a Broadway play in 1914. But when Fox finally made the musical in 1954, Leslie Caron was cast.

Gaynor was interviewed by Katherine Albert in the June issue of *Photoplay*: In the article "Hollywood's Young Unmarrieds," she commented on her first date and her fiancé, and said that members of her generation were allowed too much freedom.

On August 7, it was announced that Gaynor would play one of the title roles in *Sally, Irene and Mary*, which Fred Kohlmar would produce for Fox. This film would have no relation to the 1922 Broadway musical, the MGM film of 1925 or the Fox musical of 1938: There would be a fresh book written by Bess Taffel and a completely new score. Gaynor, June Haver and Gloria DeHaven would star as a model, a secretary and a chorus girl. On August 16, it was reported that Gaynor would play a role first played on screen by Janet Gaynor, the farmer's wife in Fox's new musical version of *The Farmer Takes a Wife*. But the role was essayed by Betty Grable in the film, made in 1952.

On August 22, it was announced Gaynor would star in the Fox musical *The I Don't Care Girl*, the story of the life and times of entertainer Eva Tanguay. George Jessel was set to produce and to supply the original story outline from which Walter Bullock would write the screenplay. Jessel would also get credit for writing the lyrics for two songs, and play a theatrical producer in the film.

2. 20th Century–Fox

Fox's Technicolor musical biography *The I Don't Care Girl* (working title: *I Don't Care*) was scripted by Walter Bullock and directed by Lloyd Bacon.. Production began on October 10, 1951, and ran until late November; additional dance sequences were shot in the subsequent months. Gaynor, top-billed above the title, performs in nine numbers: "Kiss Me My Honey, Kiss Me" (music by Ted Snyder, lyrics by Irving Berlin, sung with Bob Graham), singing and dancing "On the Mississippi" (music by Harry Carroll and Arthur Fields, lyrics by Ballard MacDonald), "Pretty Baby" (music by Tony Jackson and Egbert Van Alstyne, lyrics by Gus Kahn, sung and danced with David Wayne), singing and dancing "I Don't Care" (music by Harry O. Sutton, lyrics by Jean Lenox), "Little Fugue in G minor, BWV 578" (by Johann Sebastian Bach, leading up to "The Johnson Rag" by Jack Lawrence, Guy H. Hall and Henry Kleinkauf, sung and danced with Oscar Levant and chorus boys), dancing in a montage for an unknown number for the Ziegfeld Follies, dancing in a reprise of "I Don't Care" with chorus boys, singing "Here Comes Love Again" (music by Eliot Daniel and lyrics by George Jessel) and "The Beale Street Blues" (by W.C. Handy, sung and danced with Bob Graham and Gwen Verdon in the chorus).

The film had two dance directors for Gaynor's numbers, Seymour Felix and Jack Cole. Felix is credited with "Pretty Baby" and "I Don't Care" though Glenn Loney (in his book *Unsung Genius: The Passion of Dancer Choreographer Jack Cole*) claims that both the original and the reprise of "I Don't Care" were done by Cole. Felix also presumably staged "Kiss Me My Honey, Kiss Me" and "On the Mississippi." Cole is credited with "I Don't Care," "The Beale Street Blues" and "The Johnson Rag." "The Johnson Rag" is notable as Gaynor strips from a black-and-white floor-length Italian Renaissance costume with a large feathered hat, down to her underwear and a horns headdress as she does synchronized jazz dancing. The best Cole number is perhaps the "I Don't Care" reprise. This is Cole surrealism, with Gaynor dressed in a leotard with large black ostrich feathers and matching headdress, hugging two cats in a mirror, walking an incline which turns into a train track, jumping into a pool, and backed by chorus boys dressed in black suits and hats. After an explosion, Gaynor is seen in a red version of the same outfit with feathers, climbing a ladder and kissing a fireman surrounded by fire.

The role sees her threaten Ed (David Wayne) with her shoe, pour coffee over the head of Larry Woods (Bob Graham), interact with a goat, kiss Larry, play a tambourine, throw a lamp at Stella Forrest

(Hazel Brooks) and throw a vase at Charles (Oscar Levant). When Larry sings "As Long as You Care (I Don't Care)," director Bacon has Eva stand with her back to him so that Gaynor's back has to do the reacting. Gaynor makes Eva funny. Her singing voice here is less polished, perhaps to sound like the real Eva whose famous song has her admit that her voice "may sound funny." The film's costumes by Renie include a leather-print coat with a brown high fur collar and wrists.

The movie's release was delayed until January 14, 1953. The taglines included "WILD and WONDERFUL Musical Hit!" and "The Wild and Wonderful Musical About the BAD Girl of Show Business!" It was not a box office success but was praised by Tony Thomas and Aubrey Solomon in *The Films of 20th Century–Fox*.

According to the *Variety* review, the film's short running time and lack of continuity are due to half of the footage shot being scrapped. One source claims that Jack Cole was brought onto the film because Darryl F. Zanuck was unhappy with how Seymour Felix had staged the musical numbers. Gaynor said Felix had been hired because he had known Eva Tanguay.

Gaynor admitted to not knowing much about Eva Tanguay before making the film. At her first rehearsal with Cole, Gaynor arrived wearing her ballet shoes, tights and the little dress she had made. But Cole's girl dancers were dressed in turtleneck sweaters (tucked under the bra to expose the midriff), Levis and tennis shoes and socks. Cole didn't intimidate her though his assistant Gwen Verdon did. Verdon showed Cole a whole new side of dancing and made him an even more brilliant choreographer and innovator. Verdon danced for Cole and then she taught Gaynor. Cole was the kind of choreographer who would talk to the dancer as she learned the steps. Gaynor loved working with him and he taught her many things. Cole really made her a dancer. Glenn Loney wrote in his book that Gaynor was so grateful to Cole that she wrote him a note. He had spoiled her for anyone else and she requested that he ask for her on his next film.

The "I Don't Care" reprise headdress weighed 15 pounds. While filming the number, Gaynor slid off the 16-foot platform; the feathery costume cushioned the fall. The costume had not been fireproofed, unlike everything else on the set, though she was unharmed by the flames featured in the title number. Doing "The Beale Street Blues," Gaynor fell on her back while descending a flight of stairs. The dive into the pool was done by Verdon.

Portrait of Mitzi Gaynor in *The I Don't Care Girl* (1953).

Oscar Levant commented on Fox's publicity talking her up as a stripper without removing clothes, with Levant saying there was nothing wrong with being an exhibitionist if you've got something to exhibit.

Gaynor was voted the top female favorite among the new stars in *Photoplay* magazine's "Choose Your Star" contest. Gaynor said the vote was such a surprise that for the first time in her life she was left speechless.

Her next film was Fox's black-and-white romantic comedy *We're Not Married!* (1952), shot from December 10 to late January 1952. The screenplay was by producer Nunnally Johnson, adapted by Dwight Taylor from a story by Gina Kaus and Jay Dratler. Under the direction of Edmund Goulding, five separate stories told of couples who learn that they are not legally married. Gaynor, billed ninth, plays a supporting role: Patricia "Patsy" Reynolds Fisher, a stenographer from Richmond, Virginia, is desperate to re-marry departing army soldier Wilson Boswell "Willie" Fisher (Eddie Bracken) to legitimize her coming baby. Willie is the focus of the episode and walks with a deliberate wiggle. Patsy misinterprets the interest of Chaplain Hall (Selmer Jackson) in her and gets off a funny line, "Aren't you alittle old for this kind of cruising?" She wears a head scarf by costumer Elios Jenssen.

The film was released on July 11, 1952, with the taglines "What embarrassment when we discover…" and "It's a riot when all of us discover…" A box office success, it was praised by Bosley Crowther in *The New York Times* and Tony Thomas and Aubrey Solomon in *The Films of 20th Century–Fox*.

Matthew Kennedy's *Edmund Goulding's Dark Victory: Hollywood's Genius Bad Boy* reports that Bracken worked two weeks on the film, presumably the same as Gaynor. Bracken said that Goulding was wonderful to her. He added that he loved Gaynor, describing her as wonderful, vivacious, full of fun, a lady—and very gullible.

On January 24, it was reported that Gaynor would play the title role in a revival of *Sally*, the Jerome Kern-Guy Bolton musical comedy with lyrics by P.G. Wodehouse and Clifford Grey. It would be staged for the West Coast and then on Broadway by Edwin Lester. It would play at the playhouses of the Los Angeles and San Francisco Light Opera Associations for eight weeks from April 21, with a limited run on Broadway if the productions came off well. Lester was also mulling a presentation in Dallas. Fox would allow her to do the shows as Lester had an option on her acting services for six months. The musical was originally produced by Florenz Ziegfeld in 1920 with Marilyn Miller as Sally.

On March 14, it was reported that the Association show with Gaynor would now be a restaging of *Jollyanna* from August 11 in San

2. 20th Century–Fox

Francisco and from September 8 in Los Angeles (and possibly for a week at the Dallas State Fair). The E.Y. Harburg—Fred Saidy—Sammy Fain musical formerly known as *Flahooley* flopped on Broadway the previous year, running from May 14 to June 15 at the Broadhurst Theatre. Gaynor would play the part of Sandy, created by Barbara Cook. Gaynor had an arrangement to leave her Fox contract on 90 days' notice for a six-month appearance. While her engagement in the musical was thus far limited to the California presentations, it was entirely conceivable that a way would be found to extend her run in the show.

On January 26, with Gaynor in attendance at the Foreign Press Awards in Los Angeles. she was named Best Young Box Office Personality and given the Silver Henrietta Award.

Her next film was Fox's Technicolor musical comedy *Damon Runyon's Bloodhounds of Broadway* (1952), produced by George Jessel from April 28 to late May 1952. The screenplay was an adaptation of a story by an uncredited Runyon. Director Harmon Jones' film focused on calculating New York bookie Robert "Numbers" Foster (Scott Brady), who hires 20-year-old singer-dancer Emily Ann Stackerlee (Gaynor) to work in his nightclub. Gaynor is top-billed but plays a subordinate role to Brady. We have to wait 15 minutes to see Gaynor; she is first heard singing "In the Sweet By and By" (by Samuel F. Bennett and J.P. Webster) at the funeral of her grandpappy. She has hair extensions for pigtails and speaks with a Southern accent since the character hails from Georgia.

Gaynor performs eight other numbers: "Cindy" by Paul Francis Webster and Harry Revel, singing and dancing with Little Elida (Sharon Baird); singing "Bye Low" by Eliot Daniel; singing and dancing "I've Got a Feelin' You're Foolin'" (music by Nacio Herb Brown, lyrics by Arthur Freed) with Mitzi Green and Richard Allan; dancing in a rehearsal montage; singing and dancing "Eighty Miles Outside of Atlanta" by Jimmy McHugh and Harold Adamson with chorus boys; "I Wish I Knew" (music by Harry Warren, lyrics by Mack Gordon, sung and danced with Richard Allan and chorus boys), singing a reprise of "I Wish I Knew," and "Jack O'Diamonds" by Ben Oakland and Paul Webster, sung and danced with chorus boys and girls. Her best showcase may be "Eighty Miles Outside of Atlanta": Emily Ann parodies herself as a hillbilly who wears a torn dress, sings off-key and has the bloodhounds on stage, then pulls away her pigtails and dances barefoot with the chorus boys. In the campy "I Wish I Knew," Gaynor

Lobby card for *Bloodhounds of Broadway* (1952).

is windswept on stage and the chorus boys wear what look like blue sunglasses.

Emily Ann evolves from a barefoot hillbilly to a New York sophisticate with shoulder-length hair and shoes but clothes that are still a touch gauche compared to the glamor wardrobe of Yvonne Dugan (Marguerite Chapman). The role also has Gaynor interact with dogs and a child (Sharon Baird), kiss and be kissed by Numbers (Brady), be slapped by Yvonne, throw Yvonne over her shoulder (perhaps this was a stunt double), cry and scream. Her acting is mannered but there is a new maturity in the emotions. The film's costumes were by Travilla.

The film was released on November 14 with taglines that included "The Screen's Big Broadway Musical—with all the fabulous Damon Runyon Guys and Dolls." It was praised by Bosley Crowther in *The New York Times*, who wrote that Gaynor's presence was most winning when she danced or sang, and Tony Thomas and Aubrey Solomon in *The Films of 20th Century–Fox*. It was remade as the romantic comedy *Bloodhounds of Broadway* (1989).

2. 20th Century–Fox

George Jessel made a pitch for Fox to get Judy Garland for Emily Ann. Gaynor found the script charming. She thought Scott Brady was gorgeous, tall, funny, tough and Irish. It wasn't often that an actor could be funny and stylish. She called the director "Carmen" Jones and said the actors terrorized the man. When Gaynor asked for direction, Jones would tell her not to bother him as he was busy, and to do what she wanted. Choreographer Robert Sidney was ingenious in using things that were around the set as storage. When they had to rehearse the dances, there was no rehearsal space at Fox so a Quonset hut on Western Avenue was used. On Gaynor's first day, she arrived to find Sidney and the boys sitting at the hut's loading dock. When she introduced herself, Sidney said, "Well, Miss Pickford. What are we going to do about your big fat ass?" Gaynor replied, "Kiss it?" and the two become best friends.

Sidney said she fell on the floor laughing at his statement and that he enjoyed Gaynor's playful nature. She impressed him from the beginning and he knew she was going to be a star. She was not the typical glamor girl, but funny.

Sharon Baird reported that she had a wonderful time dancing with Gaynor. Their scene was done in one day and Baird said it was a joy.

Gaynor was profiled in the April *Photoplay* in the Liza Wilson article "They Call Her Sparkle Plenty." Readers learned that Gaynor drove a black Mercury, her favorite color was red (thus the red nail polish), collected ballerina dolls, ate everything except parsnips, and slept in gaily flowered silk nightgowns. She saved motion picture magazines and had stacks of them all over her house. If anyone whistled in her dressing room, they had to go outside, turn around three times and spit before returning. If Gaynor dropped a mirror, she swore and spat to take off the curse. Her favorite swear word was *siedemdziesiątsiedem*; that's "77" in Polish but it sounded marvelously awful and made everyone look horrified. Gaynor loved talking on the telephone while balancing on one foot and did arabesques during the conversation. She even danced when dressing. Gaynor exercised by lifting the coffee table (complete with china and knickknacks) from the floor with her toes, an act that panicked her mother every time. She and Pauline were still great pals; Gaynor felt that her mother was right about everything. Pauline wrote poems and together they were composing a song, "Little Dingle," inspired by the San Francisco cable cars. What Gaynor particularly appreciated was that Pauline was definitely not a movie mother; in fact, very few people at Fox had met her. Loving nicknames, she called her leading men Cousin or Cuz. Gaynor was always hungry on set and between takes snatched nibbles from the workmen's lunch boxes. Gregarious, bouncy and bubbling, she loved clowning and entertained with imitations and bad puns. Gaynor feared she would make dull copy.

Gaynor was again in *Photoplay* in Wynn Roberts' July article "Her Happiness Is Showing." At this time, she planned to marry Richard Brown Coyle in September. Her mother found him to be delightful. Gaynor had secured a promise from her daughter as a little girl not to marry until she was 21, which was only two months away. Pauline always knew her daughter would fall in love when she was very young and wanted Mitzi to marry a man she could be with for the rest of her life. Gaynor loved Hollywood, every star she had met, every place she had been, every film she had been in, and Richard Brown Coyle most of all.

3

Jollyanna

Gaynor was released from Fox to star as Penny in *Jollyanna* with the Civic Light Opera Association. She began rehearsals in July, saying it was a thrill to finally star in an Association show after all her appearances in the chorus. The show would open in August at the Curran Theatre in San Francisco for four weeks and moved to the Philharmonic Auditorium in Los Angeles in September. The director was Jack Donohue. The San Francisco run was something less than a hit and it was felt that it needed a first-rate dance routine for Gaynor.

The program shows that she performed in eight numbers: "A Gal Named Cinderella," "The World Is Your Balloon," "You Too Can Be a Puppet," "Jump. Chillin. Jump," "How Lucky Can You Get," "The Springtime Cometh" and a reprise of "The World Is Your Balloon." Penny's one solo number was "Scheherazade No. 1," a hip-wiggling tassel dance staged by Jack Cole which was introduced in the Los Angeles run from September 8. The costume by Jay Morley for this number and her bumps and grinds was said to set the town on its ear at the Auditorium, which doubled as a Baptist church. Gaynor reported that the church elders attended opening night and they were very nice, but someone's criticism resulted in the number being censored. This was a pity because a burlesque strip tease in nothing but a few skinny little scarves was the best part she ever had.

While Gaynor was in San Francisco with the show, two of her biggest fans, Bill and Clara French, gave her a copy of *Alice in Wonderland*. She fell in love with the married couple, who were old enough to be her parents. The Frenches joined Gaynor's fan club to keep up with her every career move. Whenever they were in Los Angeles or she was in San Francisco, they got together for dinner. The latter city became Bagdad by the Bay for Gaynor, romantic and fabulous.

Gaynor was profiled in the October issue of *Photoplay* for an article by Maxine Arnold entitled "The Strange Romance of Mitzi Gaynor." She and Richard Brown Coyle already looked married, as when they were seen celebrating holidays raking leaves and working together in her yard. Gaynor was particularly amused at how reporters assumed she would marry the day she turned 21. The wedding was postponed because Gaynor planned to be with *Jollyanna* until the middle of January and she didn't want to marry while doing a show. The plan was to take *Jollyanna* across the country and maybe to Broadway, and a husband catching up with her for a day or two wasn't Gaynor's idea of marriage. Neither was a hectic, hurried ceremony between a matinee and an evening performance. She and Richard would wait until it could be the way they had planned it. A magazine had asked her to model a wedding gown layout but, being superstitious, Gaynor refused. It was the same as when she was up for a part: Gaynor never told her loved ones for fear of jinxing it.

She and her mother had taken a week's vacation the previous year to Twenty-Nine Palms without Richard. The first two days were fun but by the third day, Gaynor was calling him long distance three times a day. Richard had a wonderful sense of humor and teased Gaynor when she dropped slang expressions picked up at the studio, like something was "real gone" or "cool." He knew how much the business meant to her and that it wasn't just about money. She always asked for two copies of a script so that they could read lines together.

The couple were living with Pauline in their rented house though in separate apartments. This added to the rumor that the marriage had secretly taken place. Gaynor explained that the apartment had been rented to Richard and his mother Min as an economic move, to help them save for the home they hoped to buy. When she and Richard spoke about living apart from the mothers when married, they joked that he would miss Pauline's cooking and Gaynor would miss Min as a canasta partner. They were an affectionate family foursome, whether playing cards or going to the movies. If it was a Gaynor film, Pauline would offer helpful comments, Min would love whatever Mitzi did, and Richard would say nothing with his fists clenched, waiting for the jury to come in.

Gaynor felt the Hollywood home was lucky: Pauline had written a television play there, and a recording company was interested in putting out an album of songs with her lyrics. After moving in, cousin

3. Jollyanna

Yvonne quit her job with an ice show and started working nonstop with a modeling agency. Yvonne's boyfriend hadn't worked in a year, then after a visit, he got a series of television shows. The house was so lucky that Gaynor didn't want to leave it.

When the planned tour of *Jollyanna* was cancelled, Gaynor appeared in a Movietone short giving the *Look* Magazine Award for Best Male Performance in a Supporting Role to Richard Burton for *My Cousin Rachel*.

She was interviewed by Jane Corwin for an article in the January 1953 *Photoplay*, "Change of Heart." The relationship with Richard was over. Gaynor now didn't feel ready for marriage, and she and her mother moved from their house to a modest apartment together. It was claimed that the engagement ended because Gaynor was wined and dined by one of the world's most charismatic billionaires and womanizers, Howard Hughes. Hughes wanted to sign her to a contract at RKO after seeing her in *Damon Runyon's Bloodhounds of Broadway*. She felt Hughes was divine—good-looking, fun and terribly generous. He gave her a diamond necklace and earrings, and recommended buying land in Las Vegas for $25 an acre and later sell them for $2 million. There was a rumor that Hughes had paid for Jack Cole to stage Gaynor's specialty number in *Jollyanna* and that he wanted to produce a lavish musical for her. It was said that the strange man had Gaynor watched 24 hours a day and, alternatively, that he stashed her away at the Sands Hotel and saw other women.

She said they were together for eight months and Gaynor thought she loved him. Gaynor also said she was madly in lust with him. But she knew it wasn't right because Hughes was too old for her, more than twice her age. He proposed with a ring but the dream of marriage soured when Gaynor learned Hughes had other fiancées. Gaynor then read about Hughes and Terry Moore's romance in the newspaper. She wanted to meet with Moore but Hughes said not to, as Moore would beat her up. But Gaynor did have lunch with Moore, and then decided to end it with Hughes. He told her to keep the engagement ring, which Gaynor did. She was angry at the betrayal but also devastated at her loss. Eddie Bracken said that Gaynor went through hell but Robert Sidney thought it was important to remember that she walked away from Hughes; she was not dismissed, as so many others had been. Gaynor was now grateful that she had not signed with RKO.

Depressed and with a stalled career, Gaynor turned to food for solace.

When she was dancing, Gaynor had no trouble losing weight but now she had stopped dancing. She ate five to six times a day, pigging out on chocolate cake and candy at four a.m. Gaynor gained 35 to 40 pounds, and now tipped the scales at 160.

On February 9, Gaynor and Jack Bean met at Harry Belafonte's opening at the Cocoanut Grove. Bean was an ambitious talent agent and advertising executive, and Belafonte was a client of the firm Jack worked for. Bean told two versions of what happened: The first is that he had a friend who had arranged to go with two girls, and Jack agreed to make it the foursome. One of the girls didn't show—Gaynor said this was her cousin, who unexpectedly fell ill—and Jack's friend was called away on business, which left him alone with her. In the second version, one of Bean's co-workers one day asked Jack if he could rumba. The agency was trying to sign Gaynor, and Jack agreed to help: He would rumba with her while the other man did the agency pitch. (She didn't sign.)

Gaynor's version is that her agent wanted her to hear Harry Belafonte, whom she assumed was an Italian singer. Gaynor dressed up in a black velvet outfit, sexily cut down the front, and was ready for drinking and dancing. Her agent had sent an escort to the Chateau Marmont where she was staying. Gaynor saw this tall, handsome, blue-eyed man, who told her he was looking for Mitzi Gaynor. She asked Jack why he didn't recognize her because Gaynor was in all the movies. He only went to foreign films. His car was a two-door Plymouth, which needed to be washed, and whose backseat was loaded with dirty clothes. When they arrived at the Grove, she stepped out and flashbulbs started going off. And then the laundry fell out of the backseat onto the ground around her feet.

It was love at first sight for Jack but for her it would take three dates. The fact that he didn't know who she was might have made the average star feel insulted, but it just made her laugh. Jack told Gaynor how attractive he found her and tried to make a good impression. But when they got up to dance and she started to lead and blow kisses, Jack leaned in. She thought he was going to say something romantic but he whispered, "You are so full of shit." Gaynor was shocked but she knew it was the truth and appreciated his honesty. Jack then whisked her away to two little jazz spots in Los Angeles.

When he called her a week later, Gaynor asked what kind of fellow Jack was, not calling sooner to say how much he had enjoyed the first

3. Jollyanna

date. Jack explained he had been out of town. Although she was seeing other men, Gaynor would talk to him on the phone at midnight after the dates for an hour.

On March 11, Gaynor was operated on for appendicitis at St. John's Hospital after having suffering two attacks. She stayed a week in hospital and recuperated another week at home. One source claimed Gaynor had received phone calls and flowers and visits from her other beaus but nothing from Jack, and this bothered her. He was supposedly out of town. Jack said he visited Gaynor every night after eight p.m., after a sympathetic nurse threw everyone else out, and this is where the couple got to know each other. Soon they became exclusive.

Jack was able to guide her through a professional crisis. By 1953, Gaynor had yet to prove herself at the box office and her Fox career was hanging by a thread. Jack said that at first she was mishandled by the studio, which put her in films with no stars or had her play roles Gaynor was too young for. Then it seemed she had no representation at all and was being paid $1500 a week to do nothing. Gaynor needed to break away from cute adolescents and become sophisticated and smart. Her curly long hair had to be cut short. The full skirts and frills, long dangling earrings and charm bracelets had to go. And she needed to reduce her post–Hughes weight.

When Gaynor and Jack were looking at fashion magazines, she admired a beautiful silver gown. He thought that would look gorgeous on her—*after* she lost some weight. It was the brutal truth and it snapped her into action. She also feared that the extra weight might mean her losing Jack's love. There was also the career, since Gaynor had played zingy, slim and pretty romantic leads and Fox would never want her back if she looked fat. With the help of masseuse Louise Long and dieting Gaynor lost 35 pounds in three months. Her dieting approach was to eat everything she wanted but only half of it. Jack also recommended that Gaynor take voice and dancing lessons. He then sent her to Fox to have lunch so she could be noticed. The first person she saw, Marilyn Monroe, commented on how thin she was.

On May 22, it was reported that Gaynor was considering appearing opposite Mickey Rooney in a Broadway musical comedy, *Ankles Away*, to be produced by Frank Finklehoff. The plot was conceived by Guy Bolton and Eddie Davis with melodies composed by Harry Warren and lyrics by Johnny Mercer. Rehearsals were expected to get underway in late September or October. Michael Kidd had been approached to be the choreographer. Also on May 22, it was announced that she would be in the cast of the Fox musical *There's No Business Like Show Business*, which would start shooting in July.

Television was clamoring for her but Fox wouldn't allow it. With production of the musical delayed, Jack was successful in getting a loan to independent producer Leonard Goldstein for a Western. Jack thought this could show she could be a woman men would fight for. On July 23, it was announced that Gaynor was in the cast of the Technicolor outdoor drama *Three Young Texans*, to be made during August. It would be photographed in and around Laredo.

Director Henry Levin's *Three Young Texans* (1954) was made by the independent company Panoramic Productions but financed and distributed by Fox. Interiors were shot at RKO-Pathe in Hollywood. The film was in production from mid–August to late September. The screenplay was by Gerald Drayson Adams from a story by William MacLeod Raine. The young Texans are cowgirl Rusty Blair (Gaynor) and cowhands Tony Ballew (Keefe Brasselle) and Johnny Coly (Jeffrey Hunter). She is top-billed over the title although Hunter appears in more scenes than she does. Her hair was worn in a new short style with sculptured bangs. Costumes by Travilla included jeans and denim male drag. The role sees Rusty ride a horse, handle a rifle, throw a bucket of water over the fighting Tony and Johnny, dance with Tony and Johnny, and kick over Sheriff Carter (Dan Riss). Unfortunately, her character has little of consequence to do.

The film was released on April 12, 1954, with the tagline "Living! Loving! Fighting!" It was lambasted by Oscar Godbout of *The New York Times*.

Gaynor said riding a horse made her butt hurt, so the wrangler gave her some salve to apply. Despite the report that Jack had engineered her loan for the film, she was angry that Fox agreed to it. Gaynor had never been in a film that cost less than a million dollars and now she was in this horse opera. They had to spend $1000 to teach Gaynor how to ride.

Gaynor was a guest on the September 13 episode of the ABC-TV musical comedy series *The George Jessel Show*. It was directed by Stuart W. Phelps. Gaynor sang and danced and wore one of Marilyn Monroe's dresses, which had to be adjusted for her because it was too big.

In November, Gaynor performed her "Scheherazade" dance from *Jollyanna* at the Mocambo for the annual Press Photographer's

3. *Jollyanna*

Lobby card for *Three Young Texans* (1954), with Gaynor (center) in male drag.

Costume Ball. In the December issue of *Photoplay* she was interviewed by Pauline Swanson for an article entitled "Mitzi Made Her Mind Up." It detailed her physical and psychological change. Gaynor now lived with her mother in a modern penthouse. Moving from the nine-room house into six rooms had been a problem, with one room bulging with cartons of old photographs and clippings, mementos of old tours and old costumes. But other areas featured big furniture of modern design, vases of bright flowers and a streamlined fireplace. There was also a whole wall of ceiling-to-floor windows overlooking a canopied terrace. She and Jack gave parties on the terrace and for the first time Gaynor was really in love. They weren't engaged and hadn't set a date for marriage, but the couple was eying the Christmas holiday season. Romantically, her personal revolution had been a brilliant success, and it was also paying off professionally.

It was reported that a La Jolla summer theater wanted her for the part of Sally Bowles in the John Van Druten play *I Am a Camera*. Gaynor had to refuse but was happy that they thought she could do it.

In Las Vegas, a top casino had offered her a fabulous sum to make a nightclub appearance. The Palace in New York wanted Gaynor too. It seemed that Marilyn Monroe was not the only person who had noticed that "sweet little Mitzi" had changed.

In 1953, she received an offer to tour England, France and Italy with a musical show. Fox turned it down.

On February 25, 1954, Gaynor was photographed with Los Angeles Rams football star Elroy "Crazylegs" Hirsch for a display of their legs, which were well known for different reasons. In February, she attended a party held by Darryl F. Zanuck at Ciro's for his daughter and Terry Moore. For the Oriental theme, Gaynor donned a coolie hat and mini-sarong.

In the February *Photoplay*, Gaynor gave an impertinent interview to Mike Connolly. Lunching at Scandia on the Sunset Strip, she rattled on about her boyfriend, new songs, Oscar contenders and plans for a Las Vegas nightclub appearance. She also recalled that at a party when she was 16, she spotted a schoolmate and ran up to greet her, but the girl cut her dead. It was as though a knife had been plunged into Gaynor's heart, and henceforth she was timid and shy. It was a long struggle to overcome it and Gaynor wasn't really over it yet. It took her an awfully long time before she could even say hello to anyone and even then they had to greet her first. Gaynor had to force herself to go to parties where she would sit in corners. If anyone tried to talk to her, Gaynor would look away. If they asked what the problem was, particularly when it was someone she had spoken to before, Gaynor would lie that she was near-sighted.

Jack helped crack the shell. There was never a dull moment with him. Through Jack, and a few good friends, Gaynor had learned to pay more attention to other people and less to herself. She likened it to giving a party. If you had a good time at your own party, your guests would feel it and have a ball. When Gaynor was doing *Jollyanna*, if she sang the daylights out of every song the audience went right along with her. But if Gaynor dogged it, they were apathetic. When she got on the subject of big church weddings, her vehemence had several Scandia diners turn around to stare, so Gaynor asked Connolly if they could leave. She blushed shyly like Gaynor used to.

Fox executives took note of her new, more sophisticated image. She was tapped to appear in *Pink Tights*, a musical with a score by Jule Styne and Sammy Cahn, to star Marilyn Monroe, Frank Sinatra and

3. Jollyanna

Dan Dailey. But after Monroe refused the role and Sinatra walked out on the project, the film was abandoned.

Producer Sol C. Siegel's *There's No Business Like Show Business* started rehearsals in March and shot from mid–May to August 27. The screenplay was by Phoebe and Henry Ephron from a story by Lamar Trotti, and the director was Walter Lang. The songs are all by Irving Berlin. The story centered on vaudeville stars Molly (Ethel Merman) and Terry (Dan Dailey) Donahue. Gaynor, billed sixth, plays the role of their daughter Katie or Katy (the name is spelled two ways on marquees).

She performs in seven numbers: singing and dancing "Alexander's Ragtime Band" with Merman, Dailey, Donald O'Connor, Johnnie Ray and chorus; singing and dancing "When the Midnight Choo-Choo Leaves for Alabam'" with O'Connor (she parodies Ethel Merman); singing in the chorus for "If You Believe," performed by Johnnie Ray; singing and dancing "Lazy" with Monroe and O'Connor; singing and dancing "A Sailor's Not a Sailor ('Till a Sailor's Been Tattooed)" with Merman with the both of them in drag and chorus; singing a reprise of "Alexander's Ragtime Band" with Merman, Dailey, O'Connor and Ray, and singing the title song with Merman, Dailey, O'Connor, Ray, Monroe and chorus. Gaynor's best solo opportunity is with the first extended version of "Alexander's Ragtime Band," which she sings with a French accent. The film's costumes are by Miles White and Travilla; the musical numbers were staged by Robert Alton. An uncredited Jack Cole did Monroe's "Heat Wave." Gaynor gets to do some comedy; for example, putting two glasses on the hands of a nightclub patron who is trying to get her drunk.

The film was released on December 16, 1954, with the tagline "With Love and Kisses from 20th Century–Fox.... Straight from the Shoulder, Right from the Heart Comes ... The Musicavalcade and the Personal Story of the Greatest Business on Earth!" It was not a box office success but received Academy Award nominations for Writing, Costume Design and Music. Abel in *Variety* wrote that Gaynor was impressive. In *5001 Nights at the Movies*, Pauline Kael wrote that Gaynor had a gleeful bounciness.

Gaynor also sang and danced in a cut number, "Anything You Can Do," with Merman, Dailey and O'Connor. Footage of the number can be seen in the 1999 documentary *Hidden Hollywood: Treasures From the 20th Century–Fox Vaults*.

June Haver been another candidate for the part of Katie. Michelle Vogel claims in her book *Marilyn Monroe: Her Films, Her Life* that during production, Gaynor sprained her ankle and was unable to dance for several days.

Gaynor facetiously said she hated Monroe, who kept flirting with Jack. Gaynor sensed that the studio was now focusing on Monroe as their future star; Mitzi believed she had more talent and could do more things than Monroe, but she wasn't as sexy or buxom. Gaynor reported that she and fellow Fox contractees Anne Baxter and Anne Bancroft dished in the mornings in the makeup room. Monroe would arrive unbathed and looking terrible, with the previous night's makeup smeared over her face. The three were appalled and amused by Monroe's lack of professionalism (often being late) and her failure to look her best. Gaynor didn't realize that Monroe was suffering—going through a divorce from Joe DiMaggio, consulting a psychoanalyst, and being up all night learning her lines as she began to create Marilyn Monroe. Gaynor claimed that in her career she never worked with a stinker—but that Monroe *was* a pain in the ass (though she stole the film).

Monroe knew what she wanted and knew how to get it—but it killed her. On set, Gaynor and Merman would sing and dance and smoke and dish. She and O'Connor would tell jokes. But Monroe stayed in her dressing room with her entourage. If the entourage came out without her, the company knew there was a problem. Gaynor said Monroe became frightened and more vulnerable. Ultimately she thought Monroe had a very unhappy life because there was no one to understand her.

Monroe's odd behavior—hiding in her dressing room, leaving the set and then returning, saying she was confused—fortified the bond between Gaynor and Merman. When Gaynor met Merman for the first time, Merman proceeded to tell her the dirtiest joke Gaynor had ever heard. Bob Thomas in *I Got Rhythm!: The Ethel Merman Story* recounts the joke. "Did you hear about the two maids who were sitting on a porch? One of them asked do you remember the minuet and the other replied, Hell I don't even remember the men I fucked." Gaynor later refused to repeat the joke in public but she gave the punchline as "Kiss it? I can kiss it myself" which seems to be a different joke. Gaynor and Merman became fast friends, bonding as girls from "The Theatah." Merman called her Mitzallah, playing a faux Jewish mother, saying they were like mother and daughter. Gaynor

3. Jollyanna

said Merman was a New Yorker's dream of what a woman should be: brassy, proud, with a wonderful sense of humor. Merman wrote in her 1979 autobiography *Merman* that Gaynor called her Mom in the film and off the set.

Merman supposedly chafed at Monroe's constant tardiness and over-reliance on her acting coach, Natasha Lytess, instead of director Walter Lang. To Merman and Gaynor, acting was Just Get the Lines Out, Honey. They would go to lunch together and dish dirt about everybody. One day the gifted mimic Gaynor did an impression of Monroe—her chest thrust out and mouth open as she walked into the commissary or speaking with her breathy soft feminine voice and looking with dewy eyes. Merman then did an impression of Gaynor doing an impression of Monroe.

Merman reported that, when the film premiered in Denver, Gaynor and Jack stayed with her. After that when Merman would go to Hollywood, Gaynor always gave a party for Merman at her home. The friendship was said to last over 20 years, documented in Merman's

Lobby card for *There's No Business Like Show Business* (1954).

scrapbooks through dozens of affectionate notes and telegrams. Merman in turn sent Gaynor telegrams congratulating her on her own shows and various successes.

Gaynor reported that Donald O'Connor also got frustrated with Monroe when they did the "Lazy" number and eventually walked off the set, saying to call him when she knew what to do. Gaynor found O'Connor terribly attractive and adorable. He was very masculine, an extraordinary dancer with gorgeous lines. O'Connor was clean and graceful and at the same time he could be funny. She loved him and they enjoyed working together. Gaynor believed his remarkable talent was not fully utilized. According to O'Connor, Mitzi loved to laugh and have fun.

Gaynor reported that Johnnie Ray was hard of hearing so if there was ever a brouhaha, he would pull out his hearing aids and start to read the newspaper.

An April 16 *Hollywood Reporter* item announced that Gaynor had been released from her Fox contract, at her request, so that she could pursue a nightclub and Broadway career. One source claims that Jack gave her the courage to ask for a release and start a freelance career, which was what she wanted. Another source said that the news came two weeks into the shoot; Gaynor stated it arrived while the film was in rehearsals. Gaynor was shocked because she had never lost a job before.

Jack told Gaynor that they were going to get married; after that, if she wanted to quit the business, it wouldn't bother him. But if Gaynor thought she had something to contribute to show business, then it was time to start to work on it.

The studio saw how good Gaynor was in the *No Business Like Show Business* rushes and her part was beefed up; every day she got another page with something more to do. One addition was her solo part of the "Alexander's Ragtime Band" extended number. Jack advised her to be a trooper and be better than she had ever been in her life. Gaynor was reluctant, angry over being fired, but followed his instructions, which included later honoring the signed agreement to publicize the film when it was released. She also reported that producer Sol Siegel wanted to put her name up for a Best Supporting Actress Academy Award nomination though he didn't. Gaynor was given a going away party at Fox and was sad to leave. It had been the happiest time of her life and the studio was like a family. She couldn't wait to go to work

3. Jollyanna

every day and became known as Rita Rehearsal because she couldn't wait to get to the next project. But now it was over.

Jack approached Mitchell Leisen, producer of *The 26th Annual Academy Awards*, and arranged to have Gaynor perform. This show was held on March 25, 1954, simultaneously at the Pantages Theater in Hollywood and the Century Theater in New York and broadcast on NBC. The Hollywood director was William A. Bennington and the New York director was Grey Lockwood. With Donald O'Connor, Gaynor sang and danced the title song from the independent romantic comedy *The Moon Is Blue* (1953) by Herschel Burke Gilbert and Sylvia Fine, a Best Song nominee.

In May, Gaynor attended the opening of Ciro's. She and Jack held a blind date party (covered in the July *Photoplay*) with guests including Terry Moore and Hugh O'Brian. *Photoplay* reported that there was a new Hollywood parlor game called "When Will Mitzi Marry Jack?" There were rumors that the romance had chilled and was being reheated for publicity purposes, and it would end in a surprise flight to Las Vegas with her marrying someone else. Jack would not be cajoled or hurried into proposing. He believed that you did not marry until you were prepared to assume the responsibility of a household. He was afraid of the perils of being married to a glamor girl but mostly wanted to establish his public relations company and have a successful career of his own.

Mitzi and Jack had to make adjustments for each other. Gaynor smoked and Jack did not so he would do the rounds of emptying ashtrays as rapidly as she used them. Gaynor was a morning person and he was not. She was volatile and Jack had both feet on the ground. They were opposites that attracted and complemented each other. Jack convinced her to set something aside every month for financial security. She called him Daddy and he called her Yummy.

Before becoming an agent and public relations executive, Jack was a psychologist; Gaynor said he was her conscience. When she got lazy, Jack would tear into her, saying all the things her own conscience should say. He also gave her a new attitude toward work. If Gaynor complained about being tired after a strenuous dance rehearsal, Jack would withhold his sympathy. Dancing was her business. She had trained for it and knew her own capabilities in terms of the time you spend on each session and the effort needed to go into it. So Gaynor should guide herself accordingly.

Mitzi Gaynor

Gaynor had wanted to be in the movie *Oklahoma!* (1955), produced by Rodgers & Hammerstein Pictures and distributed by RKO. There are two versions as to what happened. The first is that Jack thought Gaynor would have been wonderful as Ado Annie so she went to see the film's director Fred Zinnemann. He told her they had already signed Gloria Grahame. Gaynor was outraged at this casting, though when she saw the film, she believed Grahame did a good job. The second version is that Zinnemann wanted Gaynor and had asked Fox when she was still under contract to them. They refused to loan her. Casting was said to have taken place in April when Gaynor was shooting *There's No Business Like Show Business*. Fox's refusal to loan her, despite their knowing they would soon cut Gaynor loose, could be seen as an act of spite. But she and Jack met with some people representing Rodgers and Hammerstein, and this would later pay off for her.

Jack gave two versions of how he proposed. The first is that it happened at a party of Gaynor's friends. He tapped her on the shoulder and, when asked the question of how she would like to be married, Gaynor replied that she would like that fine. The second story is that the setting was at a restaurant where they had gone for dinner. Jack had hoped to propose under very romantic conditions with the moon gleaming overhead in a sky dotted with stars. But the dinner was a disaster—the restaurant and the service impossible. The waiter spilled things all over the table and even on Gaynor's lap. In the middle of all this confusion, Jack said he would like to marry her and she beamed back at him and said, "Wonderful."

With production of *There's No Business Like Show Business* now over, Gaynor could have lost confidence in herself. She had been under contract to Fox for four years. She was a few years older but believed she wasn't any better. The loss of her contract meant a loss of salary. But with strong guidance from Jack, she kept her profile high.

On September 4, Jack gave her a star sapphire ring for her birthday and because sapphire was her birthstone. On the 29th, they attended the world premiere of the Warner Bros.' *A Star Is Born* at the Pantages Theater in Hollywood and broadcast by NBC as a television news special. She appears wearing a white-colored fur. Gaynor tells emcee Jack Carson she has already seen the film and thought it was wonderful and that he was one of the best things in it.

Gaynor re-teamed with Donald O'Connor, singing and dancing in

3. *Jollyanna*

the October 9 episode of his NBC musical comedy series *Here Comes Donald*. The show had multiple writers and was directed by O'Connor. The choreographer was Louis Da Pron.

Gaynor was seen in the documentary *Jamboree,* released October 15, 1954. Made by the Boy Scouts of America, it was directed by Willis Goldbeck, Paul Burnford and D. Ross Lederman.

4

Marriage

Gaynor's wedding, set for November 18, was to be held at the San Francisco home of Bill and Clara French, her biggest fans. At first she declined the offer to have the marriage performed in their living room. There were issues with time, distance, families and studio politics, plus Gaynor didn't want her friends to go to so much trouble. But after talking it over with Jack, they decided it was actually the perfect place. Yvonne Ruby and Bob Rose were set as witnesses and a few close friends and relatives would attend. The bride's "something old" was a rose point handkerchief carried by Clara's mother on her wedding day. The "something new" was handmade lingerie. The "something borrowed" came from *There's No Business Like Show Business*—a pale blue woolen suit adorned with a pale blue fox cape-collar and matching blue horsehair hat. "Something blue" was the traditional blue garter. For luck, she had a penny in her shoe.

The couple stood before the flower-banked fireplace at 12:35 and exchanged vows and Jack placed the engraved gold band on her finger. She had a ring for him too so the minister had to start again at the beginning to deliver a double ring service. It was a happy wedding where no one, not even Pauline, shed a tear.

Gaynor reported that as Jack placed the ring on her finger, he told her, "No more lamb chops. Or duck." Jack loved her cooking and she thought that was one of the reasons he married her. But Jack said she made them too greasy. So after they were married, Gaynor never cooked either of those things for him again.

The next day, a champagne breakfast was held at the Garden Court of the Palace Hotel and that evening the couple left for New York. Their plane landed in rain and the bride's suit was drenched before she reached the terminal. (Gaynor ruined two more of her

4. Marriage

honeymoon outfits in the ensuing weeks but insisted that it was good luck.) The couple checked in at the Plaza and were swamped by congratulatory telephone calls, telegrams and flowers. Among the messages was one that there was a problem with the house they thought was leased; the owner had changed his mind. Luckily they had not moved their belongings from their respective apartments. The next morning, the couple were advised that the landlady of the property where Gaynor had been living had rented it out. The solution was for Gaynor to now move into Jack's apartment.

The next day there was more bad news from Los Angeles: His car had been involved in a crash. Then *more* bad news arrived: Jack's apartment had been rented out from under *him*. Luckily he was able to have everything moved to a newly available two-bedroom apartment where Gaynor's belongings were also moved to. Later she was glad not to take the house they thought they had wanted because, while it was elegant and comfortable, it was not for them.

They had their first married Thanksgiving dinner at the Stonehenge Inn in Connecticut. Ethel Merman threw them a party at the Stork Club in New York, where Gaynor danced with the Duke of Windsor. She would also say the location was El Morocco and that when she danced with the duke, who only came up to her chest, he nestled and hummed. She reported that when the Windsors were later in town, they asked to have dinner at her house. There was little time to plan and when Gaynor was told they would eat anything, she made them meatloaf and martinis.

Merman asked Gaynor if she would like to go to England with her to do the act they had done together in *There's No Business Like Show Business*. But Gaynor's hopes of playing London's Palladium and appearing in Glasgow and Edinburgh were dashed when Merman changed her plans.

Gaynor met her commitment of personal appearance for *There's No Business Like Show Business*. Jack insisted on being with her, not wanting to have his new wife out of his sight in the midst of New York's winter when the wolf season was at its height. She reported that this was not the kind of honeymoon where they could get to know each other since they were constantly surrounded by people.

Producers Frederick Brisson, Robert E. Griffith and Harold S. Prince offered her the role of Lola in the stage production of *Damn Yankees*. This was a new musical comedy with a book by George

Abbott (who would also direct) and Douglass Wallop, and music and lyrics by Richard Adler and Jerry Ross. Gaynor and Jack had met with the producers to discuss the project and she was surprised that her husband-manager had said no. But his reason was that he had just signed her to a four-picture deal at Paramount where Gaynor would be paid two and a half times the salary she was getting at Fox. Gwen Verdon played the *Damn Yankees* role and won the Best Performance by a Leading Actress in a Musical Tony Award (and reprised it in the 1958 film version). Gaynor told an alternative version of this story where the offer came from a phone call.

The couple traveled from New York to Detroit, and then to Minneapolis to visit with Jack's family. There they were photographed at a screening of *There's No Business Like Show Business*. Then it was on to Denver as guests of Ethel Merman and her husband on Six Acres for four days. The property was named Six Acres after Merman's husband, Robert F. Six.

Gaynor and Jack planned a real honeymoon, to include a lovely lazy trip to England on one of the *Queen*s, staying in London at Claridge's and seeing the sights. Most of all, Gaynor wanted to see Buckingham Palace and the Palladium audiences, as so many of her friends had played that world-renowned house. They also planned to sightsee all over the British Isles, with a trip across the Irish Sea to Dublin, and then visit the Continent. But then work interfered again.

On December 23, it was reported that Paramount was considering Gaynor for the musical *Anything Goes,* to co-star Donald O'Connor and Bing Crosby. But the studio had yet to have a commitment from her.

Back in Hollywood for Christmas, Mitzi and Jack went to their new apartment, which friends had prepared. Gaynor's pet extravagance was shoes but she had to sacrifice 30 pairs as well as two dozen sweaters and 18 dresses which didn't fit into the clothes closets. Neither of the couple had purchased Christmas presents so on December 24 they went shopping in Beverly Hills. They split the list of names of recipients and passed one another several times with a nod. Jack spotted a duplicate of the festoon necklace his wife had admired in the window of Bergdorf Goodman in New York and bought it. She managed her own shopping very well, buying cuff links, a cashmere sports coat and several books.

Their marriage exposed more differences between them. Her idea

4. Marriage

of the perfect remembrance was an armful of violets. He loved wine cookery. She learned about the Bean filing system: a stack of folders left on a dresser. Gaynor said that if it fell on anyone, it would crush them.

On January 4, 1955, Gaynor played the Betty Grable role in the *Lux Radio Theater* adaptation of the Fox musical romance *Mother Wore Tights* (1947). On January 8, she was back on Donald O'Connor's television series *Here Comes Donald*. The show was written by Phil Davis and Hal Fimberg and directed by O'Connor and Sidney Miller. Meanwhile, Jack's public relations business was starting to zoom.

By February 23, Gaynor committed to *Anything Goes*. The Technicolor musical romance was shot from April 7 to late June at Paramount. Sidney Sheldon wrote the screenplay, based on the play by Guy Bolton and P.G. Wodehouse (and revised by Howard Lindsay and Russell Crouse). The songs were by Cole Porter, Sammy Cahn and James Van Heusen. The material had been produced as a Broadway musical in the mid–1930s. It became a Paramount musical in 1936, an episode of the musical comedy series *Musical Comedy Time* in 1950 and an episode of *The Colgate Comedy Hour* broadcast in 1954. The new film's director was Robert Lewis. The story centered on Bill Benson (Crosby) and Ted Adams (O'Connor) who are to appear together in a Broadway show. Each man discovers the perfect leading lady.

Gaynor, billed fourth, plays the supporting role of Patsy Blair, whom Bill finds in London. She sings and dances in four Cole Porter numbers: the title song with chorus, "You're the Top" with Crosby, O'Connor and Jeanmaire, "It's De-lovely" with O'Connor, and "Blow Gabriel Blow" with Crosby, O'Connor, Jeanmaire and chorus. (She spent two weeks in rehearsal and more than a week shooting the "It's De-lovely" number.) Her best showcase is the solo title song staged by Ernie Flatt. The other musical numbers were staged by Nick Castle. Costumes by Edith Head included a pink ankle-length sleeveless dress with matching scarf, and tuxedo drag for "Blow Gabriel Blow." Patsy has kissing scenes with Steve Blair (Phil Harris) and Ted—the latter being odd, as she had played O'Connor's sibling in *There's No Business Like Show Business*.

The film's release was delayed until March 21, 1956. It was praised by *Variety* and by John Douglas Eames in *The Paramount Story*. A.H. Weiler in *The New York Times* wrote that Gaynor was a treat to the eye and ear.

During production in April, the set was visited by Thai Prime Minister Plaek Phibunsongkhram, his wife and daughter. There was a stretch when Crosby was unable to work after a kidney stone removal but he would come to the studio to watch Gaynor work out. She said that whenever he walked in, it was just like opening night and Gaynor knocked herself out. She described Crosby as a waist-up dancer and he replied, after watching her walk away in a scene, that she walked like a little brook trout going right up a stream. From then on, Gaynor was known as Brooky. Her fondest memory was the recording of the soundtrack album. Billy May did the arrangements and he arrived roaring like a bull at 8:05 a.m., still in his pajamas and slippers. They finished the session at 9:30 a.m.

The film led to close friendships with Crosby and Jeanmaire. Crosby gave Gaynor a bicycle during production and taught her how to ride it. Between scenes, he told her about his recent stay in Paris, where he had a great time. The Parisian-born Jeanmaire added fuel to Gaynor's desire to see the city she described with great affection. Jeanmaire was precisely the perfectionist that Gaynor had expected one of the most accomplished ballerinas to be, and the women got along wonderfully. Gaynor reported that Crosby had a crush on Jeanmaire but because she was pregnant, she spent a lot of time vomiting. Crosby told Gaynor that he was going to quit movies. She said that if 50 people were asked if they wanted Crosby to quit, they would say no. He asked her to test out this theory. Gaynor went outside the set and proclaimed that Crosby wanted to quit movies, and she heard back, "Good!"

Gaynor said that in this film, she brought out O'Connor's sex appeal. He was as eager to travel as Gaynor, and they talked travel between takes. Their favorite pastime was looking over travel folders.

Gaynor hoped to soon visit her Indian friends who lived in the small Catholic Mission at Pukwana in Chamberlain, South Dakota. The mission was one of Gaynor's great interests and she helped the little community when she could. In return, they sent her all sorts of mementos—mostly Saint cards—which Gaynor found inspiring. The Indian friends looked forward to her letters since they liked to hear about Hollywood. Sometimes when she was too busy to write, they sent reproachful notes—"No letter from you again."

On April 27, it was reported that Gaynor had an offers from MGM to join Frank Sinatra and Debbie Reynolds in *The Tender Trap*, from

4. Marriage

Advertisement for *Anything Goes* (1956).

Warners for *The Helen Morgan Story,* from Fox for *Can-Can* and from Columbia for *Pal Joey.* She took none of them. The June *Photoplay* reported that the Beans were house-hunting and it had to have a pool to be the central social headquarters for all their activity and friends.

Swimming was also Gaynor's favorite way of keeping her 5'6" frame down to its trim 112. The magazine also featured the Robert Emmett article "Pandemonium Reigned in Paradise" which described the Beans' wedding experience. One photograph was of Gaynor at her bridal shower, which Anne Francis and Mala Powers attended.

After finishing *Anything Goes*, a tired Gaynor looked forward to a vacation with her husband. Then she heard from Paramount executive Don Hartman that production of *The Birds and the Bees*, a remake of 1941's *The Lady Eve*, was soon to start. Gaynor thought she would be perfect for the female lead. Hartman asked to have lunch with Mitzi and Jack at the Paramount commissary, where Hartman made a proposition. They could run the schedule so that Gaynor could have three weeks off without any costume fittings or script work. Jack knew of his wife's desire to play the part. She had seen *The Lady Eve* eight times when she was eight years old and adored Barbara Stanwyck, who had played the part in the original film. In response to Hartman, Jack said that three weeks could be a lifetime. Gaynor interpreted this to mean there was time for a vacation and for her to do the part, and she bounced up and down on her chair in delight. Gaynor roared with laughter when Hartman said he felt it necessary to tell her the story of the film. Instead he was fascinated when she spent the next hour telling *him* the story down to the most minute detail.

The Technicolor *The Birds and the Bees* was shot from July 11 to September 3. One working title was *The Lady Eve*. The screenplay was by Sidney Sheldon and Preston Sturges, based on a story by Monckton Hoffe, and the director was Norman Taurog. On an ocean voyage, Jean Harris (Gaynor), a card shark, and her father Colonel Patrick Henry Harrison (David Niven), cheat George "Hotsy" Hamilton II (George Gobel) out of his money. Gaynor, second-billed after Gobel, sings and dances two numbers, both with music by Harry Warren and lyrics by Mack David: "(The Same Thing Happens with) The Birds and the Bees" with Gobel and "La Parisienne," dancing with Gobel. The role sees Jean scream, run her hand through Hotsy's hair, kiss Hotsy and Patrick, cry, speak in a French accent with some funny pronunciations, interact with children, and do some slapstick fainting. Gaynor makes Jean funny but also has some sincere moments. Costumes are by Edith Head, the musical numbers staged by Nick Castle.

The film, released on March 20, 1956, was a box office success.

4. Marriage

A.H. Weiler in *The New York Times* wrote that Gaynor made a spirited thing of her assignment although her role was basically thin.

It was reported that Gobel had asked her to play his leading lady and the switch to playing comedy opposites was just the contrast she craved. Gaynor was additionally delighted when David Niven, an A-1 performer in her book, was cast with them.

According to *Elvis' Favorite Director*, Michael A. Hoey's book on Norman Taurog, she reported sick on July 12 and was out for two days. On August 6, Gaynor recorded the songs.

Gaynor said that Paramount wanted to remake some of their other Preston Sturges comedies like *Sullivan's Travels* as musicals for Donald O'Connor and herself. She considered the oldies to be perfect movies as they were but the couple could have been very good in musical versions. But these remakes were not made.

On July 26, it was reported that producers Richard Kollmar and James W. Gardiner had invited her to head the cast of the 1956 *Ziegfeld Follies* and that she was considering the offer with much interest. Gaynor would be doing a role that required her to sing and dance to songs by Johnny Mercer and Harold Arlen. The show was scheduled to go into rehearsal in late March and possibly open at the Winter Garden in April.

In October, she was profiled in *Photoplay* in an article by Dee Phillips, "What She Goes For She Gets!" It revealed that Gaynor and Jack had taken a trip to San Francisco and Carmel. During their three weeks away, they had a ball visiting San Francisco restaurants. Gaynor had wanted to stay in a bay-view suite but discovered they were hot and noisy, with boat whistles heard on the bay all night long. In Carmel, they stopped at the fabulous Highland Inn. There they invented new nicknames: Gaynor called Jack "Son" and he called her "Mother."

Gaynor reported that many kids wrote and asked her how to get started in show business. She told them that the key was to want it more than anything and be aware of every chance to practice. Jack insisted she continue her singing lessons though Gaynor kept saying she was too busy. Finally he let her have it, saying that if Gaynor wanted to stay on top, she had to keep practicing. There were hundreds of girls taking lessons, working and praying for the day when they could take her place. This idea jarred Gaynor, who admitted to never having thought of it that way.

Gaynor's marriage was what she had always wanted. It was built on basic values like having mutual respect, laughing instead of crying, sharing the very best and worst of each other, and being comfortable and honest. Although the June *Photoplay* had reported that the couple was house-hunting, they had decided to be stay in their apartment. Gaynor wanted to try her hand at decorating a few times before starting on a home.

For their first wedding anniversary, Jack gave her a gold bracelet with a Roman numeral I dangling from a dainty chain. She vowed never to never take it off. He promised to add a new number for every year they were married. Gaynor bought him a cashmere coat. Two of Jack's buddies and their dates escorted the couple to a gala dinner at Chasen's and then on to Ciro's. Several days later, they flew to New York for a second honeymoon, staying in a spacious suite in the Hampshire Hotel. The couple bought tickets for every hit Broadway show, lunched and dined in smart restaurants, then went on to their favorite midnight spots, catching up with friends. When they got home, they felt refreshed and invigorated.

On November 25, it was reported that plans for the Broadway production of *Ziegfeld Follies*, to be headlined by Gaynor, were progressing. The producers were hoping to sign Morton DaCosta as director. On January 12, 1956, it was reported that *Ziegfeld Follies* would have a May 21 opening. But when the show began pre–Broadway tryouts in May, she was not in the cast.

It was said that Fox wanted her back for the lead in their biographical musical *The Best Things in Life Are Free* (1956) but she declined, and Sheree North was cast. Gaynor guested on the April 8 episode of TV's *The Ed Sullivan Show*, directed by John Moffit at the CBS Studios in New York. She sang "Two a Day" as a tribute to the Palace Theatre, followed by a medley of songs of the famous Palace performers Helen Morgan, Fanny Brice, Al Jolson and Judy Garland: "Over There," "I'm an Indian," "Rock-A-Bye Your Baby with a Dixie Melody" and "Somewhere Over the Rainbow."

One source has Gaynor attending the 1956 Cannes Film Festival and appearing on the French television documentary series *Reflets de Cannes* for the episode broadcast on May 2. On May 14, it was announced that she would co-star as a ballerina with Gene Kelly and Leslie Caron in *Les Girls*, which Sol C Siegel would produce for MGM.

In the May *Photoplay* article "The Bride Vanished" by Tex Maddox, Gaynor said that she believed it was only when a couple had been

4. Marriage

married more than a year that a bride become a genuine wife. She reported that as soon the honeymoon was over, she tried to become her idea of the ideal wife overnight. She had read that a husband wanted an immaculate home, which their rented furnished apartment was *not*: The previous occupants had left it coated in dust with soiled woodwork, unwashed windows and unwaxed floors. So she plunged into eight hours of scrubbing and polishing, ruining her nails, bruising her knees and exhausting herself. When Jack arrived home that night, Gaynor was triumphant. But to her dismay, he did not get the least bit excited over the results of her industry. She asked if Jack noticed the difference. He said it was nice and let it go at that. Gaynor burst into tears at the rebuff and grew hysterical. Jack consoled her with the typical male reaction that no husband found housework exciting.

Gaynor painstakingly straightened Jack's cluttered desk only to have him explode because he couldn't find a thing. Again there were tears but she again accepted it and promised to remember that Jack was not as orderly as she was. From then on, Gaynor had to force herself not to tidy up his papers when she passed them because he was content to be cheerfully disorganized.

Then there was the case of the streaked windows. They had become awful and the apartment superintendent had ignored Gaynor's pleas to wash them from the outside. She considering getting a ladder, pail and sponge and doing the job herself. Instead, she mustered up the courage to tell the super she would hire someone to do it and send him the bill. This paid off and the next morning a crew gave the whole residence a professional going-over.

She was forever experimenting with rearranging the apartment. They still lacked enough closet space for her collection of tailored suits, hats with wisps of veiling and gorgeous evening gowns. Gaynor's clothes represented her glamor, femininity and beauty. She preferred sit-down dinners to buffets because she loved to dress up. She wasn't a slave to fashion but had her own individual flair. Gaynor also liked to surround herself with books and fresh flowers, plus paintings on the walls.

Her cooking was another issue which Gaynor expected would charm and delight. She loved to prepare unusual and exciting dishes, many of which she had learned from her parents. Jack had a fine appetite, and while he might comment favorably about the exotic concoctions, he expressed his hope for a hamburger someday soon.

Funnily enough, while being a perpetual worrier, she had never fretted about finances. When she met Jack, she had three agents and was obliged to pay commissions to them all. So he took over as her personal representative though Gaynor still had a manager and a lawyer to handle the details. She now read and understood all the fine print in her contracts. The new budget also allowed her to drive a Cadillac convertible.

Another compromise came over Gaynor's love of music. She would blast rock'n'roll and opera when at home doing the housework. But when she had five radios blaring the same daytime radio drama, Jack snapped off the nearest one so he could read.

Gaynor admitted to being hypercritical about her work. She was not good on the stage until she had done at least a dozen performances. And she wanted to see every single movie, even the most dismal, to find out what *not* to do as well as what might be a step up. Gaynor had received a number of tempting Broadway bids which she greatly appreciated. There was a good possibility of staging *An Evening with Mitzi Gaynor* and she could write her own ticket on television. But Gaynor put movies first.

The Beans had the travel bug. Gaynor had never been across an ocean, and the prospect was attractive to her. She wanted to go see where history happened. Jack had been in Europe during the war, and there was much he could show her. Gaynor wanted to see the art of Europe as well as the theaters, opera, ballet, the different customs, the architecture, the scenery and the people. They would roam—drive and bicycle around. The vividness of Venice especially appealed to Gaynor.

In the August *Photoplay,* Jack wrote an article about his wife entitled "My Princess Yum Yum." He told of their first period of dating and disclosed how sometimes she took his advice and sometimes not. Gaynor was still superstitious. She never put a hat on a bed, never walked under a ladder, never talked about a deal until it was signed and delivered, never said who her co-star was going to be, until he signed. Gaynor would never start anything of great consequence when the minute hand of the clock was on the down sweep, always wanting an upbeat.

Paramount's black-and-white *The Joker Is Wild* (1957) was shot from mid–October to mid–December 1956. The director was Charles Vidor, and the screenplay was by Oscar Saul, based on an Art Cohn book that was based on the life of Joe E. Lewis, a nightclub singer and comic who was popular from the late 1920s. Frank Sinatra plays Lewis

4. Marriage

"THE JOKER IS WILD"
A Paramount Picture   In VistaVision

Jack Bean on the telephone behind Mitzi on the set of *The Joker Is Wild* (1957).

and Gaynor, second-billed, plays chorus girl Martha Stewart. She first appears 70 minutes into the 126-minute running time. Her hair is short but fuller. The role sees Gaynor dance, be kissed by Joe and Austin Mack (Eddie Albert), get married, cry and be drunk. Martha gets one funny line: Joe asks if she would say they are turning out to be like two ships that pass in the night and Martha replies, referring to his bottle of alcohol, "Well, that's a very familiar smoke stack." Gaynor has two dramatic scenes, ordering Joe's friends out of her apartment and drunkenly telling Joe she wants a divorce. The actress is quite good in the latter, mixing anger and hurt. The costumes by Edith Head include a fur-collar and hemmed coat.

The film was released on August 23, 1957, with taglines that include "His most stunning portrayal ... scarred by the Chicago mobsters who tried to run his life!" and "The Most Electric Performance That Ever Shocked and Fascinated an Audience!" A box office success, it won an Academy Award for Best Music, Original Song. The film was praised by Gene in *Variety*, who wrote that Gaynor proved she could handle herself in the acting department. *The New York Times* said Gaynor rated a bow.

Gaynor reported that in 1942, she saw Sinatra perform with the Tommy Dorsey Orchestra at Detroit's Michigan Theatre. The girl went with a boyfriend and told him that Sinatra was going to be a big star. Gaynor loved working with him because he started work at 10:30 or 11 a.m., much later than the usual start time. She found him to be very professional, and he liked to have a good time when he worked.

While making the film Gaynor met with Joshua Logan, who was going to direct the film version of *South Pacific*. She had the chance to audition for the role of a lifetime: United States Navy Ensign Nellie Forbush, a naïve Midwesterner in love with a French plantation owner during World War II. The role was originated on Broadway by Mary Martin. Logan had also directed the stage production, which began its run at the Belasco Theatre on February 2, 1949. Martin won a Tony for Best Actress in a Musical and the show won for Best Musical and in many other categories. It also won the Pulitzer Prize for Drama.

The producers of the film originally planned to have Martin and Ezio Pinza, the two leads of the Broadway cast, reprise their roles. But Pinza died suddenly in 1957, prior to the start of production. It is said that Martin still desperately wanted to repeat her performance on film. She was 35 when the show opened and was now 42, and Logan

4. Marriage

was convinced that the movie needed a sexier, younger star. Soon most of Hollywood's top actresses were vying for the part, including Debbie Reynolds, Elizabeth Taylor, Susan Hayward, Doris Day and Audrey Hepburn.

Garry McGee in his book *Doris Day: Sentimental Journey* writes that Day desperately wanted to be in it but her asking price was too high for the already costly production. Logan writes in *Movie Stars, Real People, and Me* that he had misgivings about her, fearing she would simply play herself. When Logan turned up at the same Hollywood party as Day, he hoped he might see a spontaneous side when other guests urged her to sing. But Day's refusal to do an impromptu number convinced him she just wasn't right for the role. David Kaufman writes in *Some Enchanted Evenings: The Glittering Life and Times of Mary Martin* that Day's husband and manager Martin Melcher repeatedly ratcheted up her fee, and that she had a fear of flying so was reluctant to do a film shot on location in Hawaii. Another source claims that Melcher also demanded he be made a producer on the film; the Rodgers and Hammerstein company would not agree to this.

According to Logan, Elizabeth Taylor met with him and Richard Rodgers; she looked right, slightly freckled from having been out-of-doors. But she was so intimidated by Rodgers that she couldn't make a sound when asked to sing. When Logan escorted her out and met her husband Mike Todd, Taylor proceeded to belt in full marvelous voice "I'm in Love with a Wonderful Guy." Logan returned to the composer and told him what had happened. The director thought she could sing but perhaps not well enough to do the songs herself. Rodgers refused to have Nellie dubbed and would not see Taylor again.

Gaynor doubted she would have gone after the film without her husband's support. Three years prior, Gaynor probably would have talked herself out of it. But Jack kept telling her she could do it and his enthusiasm rubbed off on her. They went after the role, with Jack relentlessly pushing until she won an audition. Logan was looking for a girl to be naïve and knuckle-headed, not too capable, not too strong, not too old and not too young, and considered (in a small town) a pretty girl. Gaynor had all that plus years of experience. A meeting was arranged with Logan in New York to discuss the role. An alternate version has Sinatra taking Gaynor to meet the director.

Gaynor told a version of the story where she met Logan to talk about playing the Japanese dancer in *Sayonara* (1957), which he was directing. But on the day of the meeting, she learned that Marlon Brando, who was playing the lead, said he would only do the film if they cast a real Asian. Gaynor thought because her eyes were slanty Hungarian she could pull it off. Miiko Taka, born in the United States to Japanese parents, was cast. Gaynor decided to meet with Logan anyway. She had dressed down for the *Sayonara* part—brown suit, hair down, plain pin, gloves and bag—and this look made Logan think she looked perfect for Nellie.

Logan writes of having been warned about her, that he would have to hold her back or she would overplay the role and bury it in cuteness. Gaynor reported that when she met with him, he greeted her with "Hello, Nellie" and spoke with her for three hours. Another source has Logan greet her with "I suppose you're here about the part of Nellie. I know you can act and dance, but can you sing?" He noticed she wore a mink coat and asked where she got it. Jack had given it to her for their anniversary and Logan advised her to make sure she told Richard Rodgers that. This was presumably so Rodgers could envision the girl as the plain Nellie Forbush who didn't wear false eyelashes, black stockings, feathers—or a mink coat. When Gaynor met with Rodgers, she wore a blue suit like a uniform, her mink coat on top of it. The composer had a cold. Offering Gaynor tea, he asked her to be "mother"—meaning, please pour the tea. Unfamiliar with the expression, she told him that she and Jack weren't planning on having children just yet. This made him laugh. Perhaps Gaynor was Nellie, after all.

The composer wanted her to sing for the show's lyricist Oscar Hammerstein. On the chosen date, she had laryngitis. One version has Gaynor meeting Hammerstein in the dark, empty auditorium of the Beverly Hills Hotel. When she lost her composure, Jack sat in the back row with his head in his hands—not in despair but praying for his wife. But suddenly her head cleared and she sang two songs, "A Cockeyed Optimist" and "I'm in Love with a Wonderful Guy." Out of the corner of Gaynor's eye, she could see Hammerstein's foot tapping in time. The ensuing performance included jumping on a table, spinning around and kicking off her shoes. Hammerstein thanked Gaynor for being a wonderful sport.

On December 14, Gaynor went to see Sinatra perform at the Sands in Las Vegas. One source claims that while in Vegas, Gaynor saw Howard Hughes. It seems unlikely that the happily married actress would

4. Marriage

have restarted her affair, especially since Hughes was marrying Jean Peters on January 12, 1957.

The Metrocolor musical comedy *Les Girls* was shot from January 3 to May at MGM. The screenplay was by John Patrick, based on a story by Vera Caspary, with songs by Cole Porter. The director was George Cukor. Gaynor replaced Cyd Charisse, who rejected the film to do the MGM musical comedy *Silk Stockings* (1957) instead. The girls of the title are former members of a Parisian dance troupe. French girl Angele Ducros (Taina Elg) sues English girl Lady Sybil Wren (Kay Kendall) over claims made in her recently published memoir. Gaynor, second-billed as American Joanne "Joy" Henderson, performs in three musical numbers: singing and dancing "Les Girls" with Gene Kelly, Kendall (dubbed by Betty Wand) and Taina Elg; singing and dancing "Ladies in Waiting" with Kendall and Elg; and dancing as Kelly sings "Why Am I So Gone (About that Gal)?" The latter is perhaps Gaynor's best showcase. She also dances with Kelly in a number that is a take-off on *The Wild One* (1953), with Kelly as the leather-clad leader of a motorcycle gang.

The role has Joy imitate Angele's French accent and get a kiss from Barry (Kelly). In one scene, she is seen with hair in curlers and feet soaking in a basin of hot water. A comic scene goes from a seductive Barry chasing Joy to Joy chasing *him* in anger and smashing a framed photo over his head. The musical numbers were staged by Jack Cole and Kelly and the costumes were provided by Orry-Kelly.

The film was released on October 3, 1957, with taglines that included "They're the most vivacious ... vexacious ... flirtatious personalities in gay Paree!" and "It's a passport to pleasure." It was a box office success and won the Academy Award for Best Costume Design and was nominated for Best Art Direction-Set Decoration and Best Sound, Recording. The film was praised by *Variety*. Bosley Crowther in *The New York Times* wrote that Gaynor showed her usual dancer's charm. Pauline Kael in *5001 Nights at the Movies* described her as a bane of 1950s movie musicals—the movie executives' idea of adorable. A sequel entitled *Les Boys* was planned but not made. The NBC-TV series *Harry's Girls* (1963-64) had a similar plot of a vaudeville troupe of three women.

Gaynor considered "Why Am I So Gone (About That Gal)?" was some of her best work. The only reason she took the film was to dance with Gene Kelly. He was gorgeous, talented and fun—and danced like

French movie card for *Les Girls* (1957).

4. Marriage

no one else. Much of his movement felt like ballet to her. Kelly was a Virgo, like Gaynor, and they completely understood each other. Making the film was a challenging and thrilling experience. Once during a particularly intense rehearsal, Kelly told her not to be recalcitrant and she replied, "I'm not, I'm Catholic." Gaynor told an alternate version of this story: In a screening room to see *The Wild One*, she asked for popcorn, which led him to make the "recalcitrant" scold.

When they danced and Kelly lifted and held her, it was as if Gaynor weighed just a few pounds. She had never danced so well in her life. Kelly liked her and knew Gaynor would do anything to please him. He was very generous, keeping the camera on her rather than himself, because she was doing something very well. Kelly's later wife Patricia Ward Kelly reported that he loved Gaynor dearly and respected her devotion to excellence in the work. They were both often injured when doing their number—she had a sprained ankle when they shot the number—but Gaynor insisted on going on with it. For this, Kelly called her a great dame.

She noted that in the scene where Leslie Phillips as Sir Gerald Wren punched Kelly, the punch was real. Cukor was shocked. Glenn Loney writes in his book on Jack Cole that Gaynor felt neglected by Cole, who focused his attention on Kendall because she was not a dancer. Kelly took the "Why Am I So Gone (About That Gal)?" number when Cole fell ill. Kendall reported that Gaynor, Kelly and Elg took her into the fold and helped her dancing enormously.

Elg said the three women got along famously with Gaynor being the sensible American who napped in her dressing room and nibbled on carrots just like Joy in the film. Gaynor lunched alone in her dressing room eating a healthy salad to preserve her slender figure. There she also studied her lines and occasionally gave interviews such as the one in the January 1958 *Photoplay*. Gaynor wanted nothing less than to become the great star that she now had the chance to be. An admiring technician commented that Gaynor was a glutton for punishment, dancing until she dropped and singing until you thought there wasn't another note to get out. Gaynor was never satisfied with anything but perfection.

She commented that Cukor spoke with an affected voice and called everyone darling. Kelly declared himself a proletariat and disappeared when Cukor got to be too much. Gaynor believed Cukor did not like her and this would seem to make him, like Marilyn Monroe, another of the exceptions to the "I never worked with a stinker" claim. He had the habit of smacking people he didn't like. Cukor would never hit her because she was the lady star, and not Kendall because she was romancing Rex Harrison, but he *would* hit the little contract player Elg. One time Leslie Phillips objected to this and Cukor told him to go away. But Phillips wouldn't leave. Gaynor only had a few scenes with Phillips but she loved him.

It was said that Cukor objected to her casting. He had come to the project late and, according to some participants, resented not having any input on the script or casting. Producer Siegel told him that he could work with Gaynor or go on suspension. Cukor stayed with the film. In his book on the director, Emanuel Levy calls Gaynor a major drawback and a colorless and inadequate actress. He quotes Cukor that she was "one of MGM's flat tires" and that she was engaged for the film after he was signed. Levy claims that Cukor wanted to quit over her casting and also because Helen Rose had initially been hired for costumes. But since his career was then at a low point, he needed the job. He *was* able to replace Rose with his friend Orry-Kelly.

Gaynor also befriended Orry-Kelly, whom she described as a crazy man. One time they were together and wanted to cross the street. He walked against the light and Gaynor told him to come back to the curb. But Orry-Kelly said that the cars wouldn't bump into them because he had a cold.

5

South Pacific

When word leaked out that Gaynor had auditioned for *South Pacific*'s Oscar Hammerstein, Hollywood gossips assumed that she was being considered for a supporting role. But Hammerstein loved Gaynor's talent and exuberance. She took a day off from filming *Les Girls* to do two screen tests for *South Pacific*. (Joshua Logan said that Gaynor was the only actress who was screen-tested.) In one, she wore a blouse and long skirt and sang "A Cockeyed Optimist." In the other, she wore a tied blouse and cut-off shorts to sing and dance "I'm in Love with a Wonderful Guy." They were both performed live, accompanied by an orchestra and shot on a makeshift set. Richard Rodgers had the second test re-done with the song at a slower tempo and in a different key. This is what made him decide that Gaynor was the one.

Gaynor's casting was kept under wraps until Rodgers and Hammerstein were ready to make an announcement. She kept reading in the trade papers that any number of different stars had been chosen for the film part—an old press agent trick.

Gaynor was taking a break from rehearsing "Why Am I So Gone (About That Gal)?" when she was stunned to get the best news of her career from Jack. When he asked how his wife was, Gaynor told him that her fanny hurt, her ankle hurt, and she was coming down with a cold, but was otherwise fine. Jack responded that he wondered what the weather was like in Hawaii in August. When she asked, "How should I know?" he told her she was going to be there to do *South Pacific*. It was reported that when Gaynor got the news, she rushed onto the set, whooping to Kay Kendall and Taina Elg, "I'm Nellie ... I'm Nellie!" Gaynor finished making *Les Girls* and then she and Jack were off to Hawaii.

Three top Hollywood glamor girls reportedly took to their beds after the announcement was made. (Judy Garland and Ginger Rogers were said to be other contenders for the part of Nellie. Patti Page related in a book that she tested for the role.) Gaynor said that what gave her the edge was that she was prepared to do a screen test, when others were not. The others said, "Look at my films." Also, her competitors may have been leading screen actresses but they did not have the same musical stage background. In addition, Gaynor sang in Mary Martin's musical keys. Logan repeats in his book what he was told by his producer friend Arthur Hornblow, Jr. It is not known where Hornblow got his information as he had never worked with Gaynor, but he said that she could be very vivacious and charming and full of sex but she had to be policed. You had to smooth the too-crinkled nose, shrink the wide-world smile and calm the rolling eyes. You had to take away the things Gaynor did that got in the way of the things she ought to do. Gaynor gave you too much for your money; you had to get what you wanted and no more.

Around this time, Gaynor was being considered for a part in the Fox musical *Mardi Gras* (1958) but Sheree North was cast instead as Eadie West.

Before the Technicolor war musical romance *South Pacific* (1958) was shot, Gaynor worked with Logan every day from eight to five for three weeks. He insisted that the cast be letter-perfect so that when they were on location, no script was needed. Principal photography took place from August 12 to October 6 on location in Hawaii and French Polynesia and at Fox. The screenplay was by Paul Osburn, adapted from the play which in turn was based on James A. Michener's *Tales of the South Pacific*. In the movie, Gaynor's hair (by Helen Turpin) is blonder and shorter than it is in the screen tests.

She performs in the following musical numbers: singing "A Cockeyed Optimist," singing "Twin Soliloquies" with Rossano Brazzi (dubbed by Giorgio Tozzi), singing "I'm Gonna Wash That Man Right Outa My Hair" with the Ken Darby Singers, singing the reprise of "Some Enchanted Evening" with Brazzi, singing and dancing "A Wonderful Guy" with the Ken Darby Singers, singing and dancing a reprise of "A Wonderful Guy" with Brazzi, singing reprises of "Twin Soliloquies" and "A Cockeyed Optimist" with Brazzi, dancing at a rehearsal to a reprise of "Bloody Mary," singing and dancing "Honey Bun" with Ray Walston and the Ken Darby Singers, singing "My Girl Back

5. South Pacific

Home" with John Kerr (dubbed by Bill Lee), singing a reprise of "Some Enchanted Evening," and singing "Dites-Moi" with Candace Lee (dubbed by Marie Greene), Warren Hsieh (dubbed by Betty Wand) and Brazzi. Gaynor's best number is perhaps "A Wonderful Guy" which she sings to-camera, despite the fact that Nellie wears eye shadow and lipstick after her shower.

Footage of Mary Martin and Ezio Pinza performing songs from the show exists as part of *General Foods 25th Anniversary Show: A Salute to Rodgers and Hammerstein*, a television special broadcast on all four U.S. networks (CBS, NBC, DuMont and ABC) on March 28, 1954. Martin sings "I'm Gonna Wash That Man Right Outa My Hair," "A Wonderful Guy" and "Some Enchanted Evening" with Pinza. While her voice is not as strong as Gaynor's, Martin seems more clownish in the "A Wonderful Guy" section. In addition, perhaps because of the disparity in height between her and Pinza, Martin comes across as more vulnerable than Gaynor.

Gaynor's film role sees her kiss Emile (Brazzi) and Luther (Walston), speak French, cry, drive a Jeep and interact with children. Her performance is relatively restrained, even when she performs "Honey Bun." Her best acting comes in the scene where Nellie tells Emile she can't marry him because his dead wife was Polynesian. Gaynor's faltering singing of a reprise of "Some Enchanted Evening" helps to show Nellie's anxiety over Emile being on his mission though the stilted lines in that scene would challenge any actress. Her costumes are by Dorothy Jeakins. Logan reported that LeRoy Prinz helped him staged the dances; Prinz staged the movement for "I'm Gonna Wash That Man Right Outa My Hair."

The film was released on March 19, 1958, with taglines that included "In the thrilling tradition of *Around the World In 80 Days*" and "There is nothing you can name that is anything like *South Pacific*." A box office success, it was praised by *Variety* who wrote that Gaynor, while no Mary Martin, was essentially very professional. Bosley Crowther in *The New York Times* said that she was excellent. It was remade as a 2001 made-for-TV movie with Glenn Close as Nellie, a 2006 *In Concert from Carnegie Hall* episode of the PBS series *Great Performances* with Reba McEntire as Nellie, and a 2010 episode of the PBS series *Live from Lincoln Center* with Kelli O'Hara as Nellie. In 2010, a new film version to star Michelle Williams as Nellie was reportedly in development.

The original road show version of the film featured 15 minutes not seen in the general release version: dialogue between Nellie and Luther about the dress he makes for her, a reduced reaction when Emile tells Nellie he killed a man, a chorus of "Some Enchanted

Mitzi Gaynor in a still for *South Pacific* (1958).

5. South Pacific

Evening," Nellie watching Emile ride away and then turn to look at the nurses at the beach before "A Wonderful Guy," Emile's surprise reprising "I'm Gonna Wash That Man Right Outa My Hair" to Nellie, etc. Another cut scene that did not even appear in the road show version is a third reprise of Nellie singing "A Wonderful Guy."

Gaynor is seen in the Making Of featurette on the Special Edition DVD of the film. We see her hair cropped under the supervision of producer Buddy Adler and Logan, and on location rehearsing and filming. We also see her surfing, boating and posing in a swimsuit for photographs.

David Kaufman writes in *Some Enchanted Evenings: The Glittering Life and Times of Mary Martin* that Logan took Gaynor to see the show in Los Angeles before he started shooting the film version. He brought her backstage to meet Martin; this upset Martin, as she was aware of the younger actress being cast in the film. Gaynor said that Martin refused to let her into the dressing room.

In his book, Logan wrote that when they pre-recorded the songs, Gaynor performed hers impeccably. Despite the warning of Arthur Hornblow, Jr., no policing was necessary. He also reported that during filming, Gaynor was fun and a true professional. The 20,000 Marines and sailors in the audience of "Honey Bun" got restless between takes so Logan had her go out and talk to them. When she ran out of stories, he had to tell them stories too.

The jumbo-size sailor suit Gaynor wore for the number was made from seven yards of regulation sailor suit fabric; three copies were made for $350 each. The outfit required a half-dozen fittings, some lasting over an hour. Each time Gaynor had to go through the dance number to see if she could move in the baggy pants. she confessed that it wasn't easy. Gaynor never imagined that so much effort would have to go into creating a costume that didn't fit.

It was reported that she performed "I'm Gonna Wash That Man Right Outa My Hair" 37 times in a day and a half. Gaynor said the multiple performances were rehearsals and each time the shampoo would sting her eyes so badly that she could hardly see. The solution was to go to the mainland and get Johnson's No More Tears baby shampoo.

Gaynor reported the day she met Rossano Brazzi, she used her best Anna Magnani accent and told him he was the most gorgeous, most handsome, greatest Latin lover in all of the movies. Brazzi answered, in his Italian accent, that he knew and then adjusted himself in the crotch. How could she not love this man who was so funny? Gaynor said Brazzi was simply wonderful to work with and wonderful off-screen as well. When they were together, she felt supported and buoyed up. Gaynor reported that everyone was starving on location since they only had cheese sandwiches to eat. Brazzi would boast what a wonderful cook his wife was and Gaynor would drool over his descriptions of pasta with rich red sauce and chicken in wine.

Every Saturday they would get a half day off and go to the beach. One time Brazzi went swimming and had to be saved by Jack. The next day in the newspapers was the story of how Brazzi had almost died; the actor was angry that the story was more about Jack being the hero.

Oscar Hammerstein felt that Gaynor was superlative in the film. He never realized her dimension as a fine young actress and he believed that her performance would be the start of a new career. Gaynor described him as a mensch, a real human being, who she felt was very much "A Cockeyed Optimist." Gaynor reported that he would stop by the set to occasionally direct. He would put his arms behind his back and point out directions with his prominent belly. After they wrapped, she gave him a gold disc with the inscription "To Your Tummy" or "I Love You Tummy."

Gaynor said the role demonstrated there was a lot more to her than just being a dancer. Her onscreen persona had been kinda jazzy, kinda sassy, kinda leggy—tits and ass in high heels. She was always the cute girl who caught the guy and then they would go off and sing and dance together. Playing Nellie changed her life and approach to acting. In the past, she would act out a part and but now she became Nellie. Gaynor felt like her, thought like her, and danced like her. She had to mask her own dance technique because Nellie only had a little dance training.

Logan commented that Gaynor was a fine, deep, serious actress, probably the most talented girl—in all directions—of anyone around in those days. Making the film seemed to her like she was back at Fox with the same hairdresser, makeup man, body makeup girl, music arrangers and d.p. Leon Shamroy, who had shot *Down Among the Sheltering Palms* and *There's No Business Like Show Business*.

Ray Walston reported that upon first meeting Gaynor, as a man, thoughts went to their lowest level. She gave everything she had—fresh every morning, right on the button, a wonderful person to work with. Walston loved her and wished Jack Bean would get lost. Regarding

5. South Pacific

their explosive director, Walston said that Logan would love you one day and hate you the next. This made you want to run instead of act. Gaynor was not spared. She said he would do line readings for the actors, and that you had to do it with the same exact inflections as him. Logan played the part, Gaynor was his ventriloquist partner Charlie McCarthy. This was another reason why they had to dub the film: because he talked them through everything.

The director's temperamental behavior was triggered partly by the pressure of high expectations for the film. After months of stressful filming, she could only hope that her hard work in the most important role of her career would silence the critics and make her one of Hollywood's biggest stars. Audiences around the world wanted to know if the film and its controversial leading lady could live up to the celebrated stage version.

Interviewed in September 1957 by Fred D. Brown for *Picturegoer*, Gaynor said her schedule at the time was a far cry from the calm days ahead she saw for herself. Career-wise, she was in greater demand than ever. She still wanted to try Broadway.

On October 13, it was reported that Gaynor was in discussions to appear in the role of an actress in a Fox film based on an original story by Curtis Harrington, and to be produced by Jerry Wald. The plot concerned a movie star filming a picture at Virginia Military Institute and her effect on three undergraduates. The men would be played by Robert Wagner, Tony Randall and Jeffrey Hunter.

Gaynor was interviewed for an article in the December 28 *Picturegoer*, "The Biggest Name of 1958," by Donovan Pedelty. She said she slept in a king-sized bed because she danced in her sleep (as well as dancing while phoning and dressing). She preferred children's nightgowns if a nightgown had to be worn; otherwise she slept in Jack's T-shirts. Gaynor slept eight hours a night when working and five hours when not. She loved Steinbeck, Strauss, jazz, ballet, cooking outdoors over charcoal, and spending hot weather in air-conditioned cinemas.

The *South Pacific* film soundtrack was reportedly released in December, prior to the film's release. Gaynor's royalties reportedly exceeded her salary on the film.

In late January, it was being reported that Gaynor had committed to appearing in one or more MGM films. Gaynor said that she expected to be asked to perform something from *South Pacific* at *The 30th Annual Academy Awards* show on March 26. Instead they asked her to introduce Vic Damone, who would sing "An Affair to Remember" (a Best Song nominee).

With *South Pacific*'s box office success, Gaynor reached the pinnacle of her career. More people would remember her from it than anything else she did. Gaynor had expected to win Academy Awards and have plays and films written for her, but this didn't happen; in fact, she would never make another film musical. But screen musicals were changing. The big-budget musicals (often adaptations of Broadway hits) were being replaced by teen-orientated rock'n'roll films. Donald O'Connor said that the studios were now uncertain of the future, unlike in the past when they seemed to know what audiences wanted. Now they were hesitant to put their money into these new kind of musicals in case they proved to be a fad that would quickly fade. Costs were rising and less films were being made. Just one or two major flops could lead to bankruptcy.

In April or May, Gaynor attended the Cannes Film Festival. She said she was there at the same time as Sophia Loren and that they endlessly laughed together. Gaynor was in the May 3 and May 11 episodes of the French TV series *Reflets de Cannes*.

On April 17, Gaynor—interviewed at London's Savoy Hotel—said this was her first trip to England. (She was sent there to promote *South Pacific*.) She now wanted to be known as an actress who could sing and dance instead of a dancer who could act and sing. On May 4, she was back in Hollywood attending a dinner honoring the Brazilian's ambassador to the United States, Ernani do Amaral Peixoto. On October 11, she opened the 1959 Mile High United Fund campaign.

Billy Wilder originally wanted Gaynor to play Sugar in the United Artists comedy *Some Like It Hot* (1959), but when Marilyn Monroe became available, he cast her instead. David Thomson writes in his book *"Have You Seen?": A Personal Introduction to 1,000 Films* that Gaynor was also on stand-by in case Monroe was unable to complete the part. But Charlotte Chandler stated in her book *Nobody's Perfect: Billy Wilder. A Personal Biography* that ultimately Gaynor was not what Wilder wanted. Ed Sikov in *On Sunset Boulevard: The Life and Times of Billy Wilder* writes that the suggestion to cast Gaynor came from United Artists, and Wilder rejected it.

On January 25, it was reported that Gaynor would appear in the United Artists film *Anniversary Waltz*, an adaptation of the Joseph Fields-Jerome Chodorov Broadway comedy (1954-55). It dealt with the

5. South Pacific

farcical aspects of a couple's fifteenth wedding anniversary celebration. Gaynor would play opposite David Niven, with Fields acting as producer, screenwriter and director.

On March 18, Gaynor guested on the live CBS-TV comedy special *The Jack Benny Hour*, shot in Hollywood. The show had multiple writers and was directed by Bud Yorkin. Gaynor performed four musical numbers: singing and dancing "A Wonderful Guy" from *South Pacific*, singing "Mr. Wonderful" by Jerry Bock and George David Weiss and Lawrence Holofcener with Benny, dancing to "There's No Business Like Show Business" with a female chorus line, then dancing with male dancers, and singing and dancing "Everybody Loves to Take a Bow" (music by Jule Styne and lyrics by Bob Hilliard) with Benny, Bob Hope and a chorus. The choreography was by Robert Sidney and costumes by George Whittaker. She is funny bantering with Benny, as when she suggests that he lacked sex appeal in his movies. She said she asked the studio to put him in *South Pacific* because she felt he would have been wonderful as the planter as she understood Benny grew rice in his swimming pool. Jack Gould in *The New York Times* wrote that Gaynor was not aided by the costumer since her clothes seemed harsh and bold in contrast with her youthful and wholesome piquancy. Gaynor said the show didn't really need her as Benny had the Marquis Chimps and Gregory Peck singing and dancing. Gaynor learned about timing from Benny.

The show's closing credits mention her new album *Mitzi*, released by Verve Records. It was arranged and conducted by Pete King and his Orchestra and featured 12 songs: "Do What You Do," "I Won't Dance," "The Nearness of You," "Cheek to Cheek," "Nobody Else But Me," "Rain," "The Thrill Is Gone," "That Old Feeling," "I Only Have Eyes for You," "Lazy," "Do It Again" and "When Your Lover Has Gone." Gaynor's vocals have a surprising amount of vibrato. Her choice of "Lazy" is interesting given how Marilyn Monroe did it in *There's No Business Like Show Business*. For the song, Gaynor speaks some of the lyrics. Her version of "Do It Again" is perhaps the most radical in its arrangement. For the most part, her vocals are tentative though it's fun to hear Gaynor sing in a lower register. She goes all-out dramatic for "When Your Lover Has Gone" with the track aided by a gorgeous musical arrangement by King.

The same year, Verve Records released *Mitzi Gaynor Sings the Lyrics of Ira Gershwin* aka *That Certain Feeling*, arranged by

Russell Garcia. This also had 12 songs: "Soon," "Half of It Dearie Blues," "Spring Again," "Gotta Have Me Go with You," "Here's What I'm Here For," "I Can't Get Started," "Treat Me Rough," "That Certain Feeling," "My Ship," "There's a Boat Dat's Leavin' Soon for New York," "Island In the West Indies" and "Isn't It a Pity." On this album, her vocals are again done with surprising vibrato but this time it seems the arrangements of Garcia are too heavy-handed. Gaynor is almost battling the orchestra to be heard. The track "Gotta Have Me Go with You" is interesting in that the tempo is slower than that performed by Judy Garland in *A Star Is Born* (1954), though it is still an up-tempo song. But then "Here's What I'm Here For," another Garland track from the film, is here done in a faster tempo. Another track with a changed tempo is "Treat Me Rough," done here in a slower tempo than as done by June Allyson in the film *Girl Crazy* (1943).

Gaynor said the albums were not a financial success. She quipped that they must have sold eight of them both, but she felt they were not bad.

Gaynor performed at *The 31st Annual Academy Awards*, held on April 6 at the Pantages Theater in Hollywood and broadcast as a television special on NBC. The show was directed by Alan Handley. She sang "There's No Business Like Show Business" wearing a Dior scarlet number rippling in fringe bought from Bergdorf Goodman. As the show was running short, Gaynor had to sing additional choruses to fill time. She reported that after finishing the number, Valentine Davies, the general chairman of the show, yelled at her backstage to go back and do it again. The song's composer Irving Berlin had only written a couple of choruses. So every time Gaynor finished the song, she had to go back to the chorus and sing it over and over again. Gaynor said she sang four choruses.

On April 16, Gaynor attended the first American tour performance of the Soviet Union's Bolshoi Ballet at New York's Metropolitan Opera House.

Her next film was the abovementioned *Anniversary Waltz*, now titled *Happy Anniversary* (1959), shot in New York in black-and-white from April 27 to mid–June. The screenplay is credited to Joseph Fields and Jerome Chodorov, based on their play, and the director was now David Miller. Second-billed Mitzi plays the leading role of Alice Walters *née* Gans, the wife of Chris (Niven). The role was originated on stage by Kitty Carlisle. Gaynor performs one song, "I Don't Regret a

5. South Pacific

Thing" (music by Robert Allen and lyrics by Al Stillman) as she dances with Niven. One source has her also singing the Allen-Stillman title song but this was not in the viewed print. The role has Gaynor play a mother for the first time. At the age of 27, she is too young to be playing a woman celebrating her thirteenth wedding anniversary, the mother of two young teenagers. The new treatment reduces the anniversary from 15 to 13 years to imply that the couple had a child before being married. The idea that they had a pre-marital sexual relationship got the film in trouble with the Motion Picture Production Code. (The role of Alice was offered to Doris Day but she or her husband Martin Melcher declined, fearing it would damage Day's pure screen image.) Niven plays Gaynor's husband here after having played her father in *The Birds and the Bees*.

The character of Alice is kissed by Chris, dances with Chris and interacts with children. Gaynor is funny, as when Alice comments that she is deliriously happy with an angry tone. She also gets a funny line: When she tells Chris of her pregnancy, he asks if she is sure, and Alice replies, "Do you want to go to the rabbit's funeral?!" Gaynor's

Mitzi Gaynor and David Niven in *Happy Anniversary* (1959).

fuller short hair is by Mary Roche; gowns are by Molly Parnis and Ben Zuckerman.

The film was released on November 10 with the taglines "At last! The First Comedy Actually Filmed in SIN-ASCOPE, The Most Exciting Process Ever Invented!" and "It bounces convention right out the window!" A box office success, it was praised by *Variety* but Bosley Crowther in *The New York Times* wrote that Gaynor and Niven behaved as if they were plastic mechanisms operated elaborately by springs.

A soundtrack album was released with Gaynor singing "I Don't Regret a Thing" and a version of the title track, which had been sung by a chorus under the opening credits. Gaynor recalled that Patty Duke, who plays Debbie Walters, was wonderful—intuitive and talented. It was a joy to work with her and with Kevin Coughlin, who plays Ockie Walters. She called Niven divine and brilliantly talented.

Duke wrote in her autobiography *Call Me Anna* that Gaynor was a lovely, bright, sunshiny person. She elaborated in her book *In the Presence of Greatness: My Sixty-Year Journey as an Actress* that there wasn't a flaw anywhere on Gaynor's skin or in her hairdo—and what a body she had! Duke learned lessons on manners and how to behave from Gaynor. She also reported that Gaynor and Niven were very witty, so there was a lot of laughter on the set. Duke said Gaynor was good to her and Kevin Coughlin—generous, complimentary to them about their work—and made them feel like equals.

Gaynor reported that during filming, Ethel Merman opened in *Gypsy* on Broadway. On May 21, opening night, Merman visited her at the New York apartment on Park Ave and 65th Street. She arrived at six p.m. when the show curtain was eight p.m. and had a steak sandwich and a glass of milk. Gaynor went to the opening of the show at the Broadway Theatre. When Merman came down the aisle to make her entrance, she said hello to Mitzi before going onto the stage.

In a May 10 *New York Times* article by Richard W. Nason, Gaynor stated that making a film in New York was no different than making one in Hollywood.

The October 19 episode of ABC-TV's *The Frank Sinatra Timex Show* was written by Johnny Bradford and directed by Bill Colleran, with choreography by Tom Hansen. Gaynor performs in five numbers: "High Hopes" (music by Jimmy Van Heusen and new lyrics by Sammy Cahn), sung with Bing Crosby, Dean Martin and Sinatra; dancing "Hurricane Mitzi" with four chorus boys and a singing

5. South Pacific

chorus; dancing to "Talk to Me" (by Eddie Snyder, Rudy Vallee and Stanley Kahan) as Sinatra sings, "Cheek to Cheek" (by Irving Berlin), sung and danced with Sinatra, Crosby and Martin; and "Won't You Come Home, Bill Bailey" (by Hughie Cannon), sung with Crosby, Martin, Sinatra and Jimmy Durante. She enters with a troop of children as their "nanna," blowing a whistle, before the troop sings "High Hopes" with the original Sammy Cahn lyrics accompanied by Sinatra. Richard F. Shepard of *The New York Times* wrote that Gaynor's dance number seemed uninspired. She claimed that they wanted to call the show *Frank Sinatra, Dean Martin and Bing Crosby Present Mitzi Gaynor*, but Timex didn't like the idea. "Hurricane Mitzi" came from the fact that Florida was full of hurricanes at the time.

Her next film was the Columbia black-and-white comedy *Surprise Package* (1960), shot under the working title *Surprise Party*. Production took place from October 12 to December 23 on locations in Greece and England and at England's Shepperton Studios. The screenplay was by Harry Kurnitz, based on a book by Art Buchwald. In director Stanley Donen's film, Nico March (Yul Brynner) is a gangster deported from the United States and sent back to the Greek island where he was born. Gaynor, second-billed, plays showgirl Gabby Rogers. She uses what sounds like a slight New York accent and her hair by Joan Smallwood is longer and worn up or in a ponytail. Gaynor sings and dances the title song (by Sammy Cahn and Jimmy Van Heusen) with Noël Coward, who plays King Pavel II.

The role sees her kissing and being kissed, crying, playing Scrabble, riding sidesaddle on a donkey, painting her toenails, running and faint. She also does some slapstick. Gaynor is funny in the scene where Gabby asks "Make a what?" when told by the hotel manager (Andreas Malandrinos) to make a curtsy when meeting the king. She also gets an entertaining monologue about how the king's crown is jinxed. Gabby's clothes by Mattli are appropriately brassy.

The film was released on September 29, 1960, with the taglines "SURPRISE! A Big Time Operator! SURPRISE! A Body-Beautiful Stripper! SURPRISE! A Continental Smoothie! SURPRISE! They Make Out on a Way-Out Grecian Island in the Prize-Package Comedy of the Year!" and "You'll enjoy this picture to the very end!" Bosley Crowther in *The New York Times* wrote that Gaynor played as if her only experience as an actress was in the third road company of the original *Gentlemen Prefer Blondes*.

Halsey Raines reported on the shoot in Rhodes, Greece, in the November 8 *New York Times*. The actors were unknown to most of the townspeople who had never seen a movie or owned telephones or radios. When shooting a scene where Brynner threw Gaynor onto the ground, children became upset and protectively gathered around her. Brynner explained that they were only acting. The couple held hands between takes to show that there were no hard feelings, but the children's reactions were the same. They cheered when this strange American game was over. This incident was captured in director Maurice Binder's comedy short *The Children of Lindos*, about the making of the film.

Gaynor liked the film but joked that she only knew three people who had seen it. She took the film because she wanted to work with Brynner and Stanley Donen. On November 6, after shooting on location was completed, the company moved to London for the interiors. Gaynor and Coward were drawn to each other. Gaynor sat with him in his dressing room and Coward regaled her with stories, a lot of them dirty. He was a classical man and a very fine thinker. He wrote some very flattering things about Gaynor in his published diaries, reporting that she was a dear to work with and that he found her charming in the film. Later there was talk of Ross Hunter doing a musical version of Coward's play *South Sea Bubble*. Coward was to write the score, and Gaynor would star. It was never made.

Gaynor reportedly told Brynner that he was the biggest ham hock in the world. For the end of production gifts, she went shopping at a London antique store and spent five pounds on a couple of framed cameos for him. When Brynner gave an interview the next day, he told reporters Gaynor had given him Hungarian museum antiquities. Coward had her read Brynner's lines off-camera to him for closeups because the man couldn't understand Brynner's heavy Russian accent. Gaynor spoke the lines in her imitation of Brynner.

Donen said that Gaynor was his first choice for the part of Gabby. Gaynor said that Donen handled the actors with his typical grand style, an incredible eye and tremendous grace.

She was a guest on ABC-TV's *The Dick Clark Show* on January 30, 1960, Gaynor performed "I Don't Regret a Thing."

It came to her that staying in Hollywood was not going to be a viable option if she wanted to remain a star. The kind of movie musicals Gaynor used to make, seemed to be finished. Once again she

5. South Pacific

Advertisement for *Surprise Package* (1960).

took Jack's advice and decided to perform live in Las Vegas, which was proving to be a profitable enterprise. She had received an offer and Jack said yes, if they gave her a piece of the hotel. This condition was rejected. But Morris Landsberg, the new owner of the Flamingo Hotel, agreed to give her a two percent share of the profits of the hotel and casino. Gaynor and Jack formed Green Isle Enterprises to produce "The Mitzi Gaynor Show." She was dubious about the venture, not wanting to compete with the booze and smoke. Landsberg offered

$40,000 a week and agreed to finance her next two films. He invited her and Jack to the March 4 Sugar Ray Robinson–Gene Fullmer prizefight, held at Vegas' Convention Centre. She said that if Fullmer won, she would do the act. He did win.

Gaynor was a presenter at *The 32nd Annual Academy Awards*, held on April 4 at the Pantages Theater. The show was written by Bill Larkin and directed by Alan Handley. Gaynor bestowed the Best Documentary Feature and Short Subject Awards.

As Rossano Brazzi's *South Pacific* co-star, she was interviewed for the *This Is Your Life* TV episode devoted to him. It aired on April 20. On July 14, Gaynor attended the funeral service for Buddy Adler at the Los Angeles Temple Israel. The 20th Century–Fox executive producer (and producer of *South Pacific*) had died on July 12 of lung cancer at age 51. She was back on *Here Comes Donald* for the October 11 episode broadcast, directed by Greg Garrison. Gaynor performed a solo dance and, with Donald O'Connor, sang and danced "All I Need Is the Girl" from the musical *Gypsy* (music by Jule Styne, lyrics by Stephen Sondheim). The episode was praised by John P. Shanley in *The New York Times*.

Gaynor attended *The 33rd Annual Academy Awards*, held at the Santa Monica Civic Auditorium on April 17, 1961. She was scheduled to interview the winners as they came offstage. But no one made it to the room where Gaynor was stationed. She placed the blame on the lack of rehearsal.

6

Las Vegas

For her Las Vegas act, Gaynor said that she invented a Broadway revue kind of show that had never been seen in Vegas. There had been men and lady singers and groups and comics. But nobody put on skits and changed costumes 20 times and did songs and dances. After her, Debbie Reynolds, Juliet Prowse and Shirley MacLaine copied the idea.

Gaynor hired Robert Sidney to stage it. (She was amused by the way Sidney spoke. To her, he sounded like Tallulah Bankhead.) She had special musical material written by Jay Livingston and Ray Evans. She performed as a good girl and as bad girls. The good girl was Nellie Forbush from *South Pacific,* who just happened to be an Arkansas native. The bad girls included a slithery 1920s tango queen, a 1930s European glamor goddess *à la* Garbo or Dietrich, and a fiery 1940s strip-teaser. Gaynor was supported by four chorus boys, hi-tech lighting and sound, and new costumes. One source reported that there would be glitzy sets, but Gaynor claimed they only used the stage scrim. Most importantly, there was a star who would sing, dance and clown. Her show ran 55 minutes.

Gaynor decided to do an out-of-town tryout and chose the nightclub The Vapors in the resort city of Hot Springs, Arkansas. Jack had heard that the club was owned by Owney Madden, who had run Harlem's Cotton Club during the 1920s. The venue seemed like a good choice as it was away from the national media and allowed her to work out any kinks before taking the show to Vegas. The fact that the club was called The Vapors was apt as the midsummer weather was hot and humid. Gaynor and Jack settled into the Velda Rose motel across the street for the act to run from May 29 to June 11.

The opening night changed her life forever. She was performing as different personas as she had always done in the past. But at other times she was just being herself, which made her extremely nervous. For the first time, as the overture played and Gaynor stood in the wings, she wondered if the audience would like her. She found out quick. She could hear the people buzzing, which was thrilling after years away from performing on stage. They had come to see her, out of love, and there was nothing like that realization for a performer.

As the show began, nobody laughed or applauded when they should have. They just sat there, and Gaynor was sure the show was a bomb. But when it ended, the audience members stood up and cheered for ten minutes. They stood on top of the bar shouting for more. At that moment, Gaynor knew this is what she wanted to do for the rest of her life.

Having shaken off her nerves with the Hot Springs run, Gaynor was now ready to make a confident Las Vegas debut on July 6. She strutted her stuff and any doubts there were about her drawing power were erased. Sidney reported that she wasn't expected to be that good but Gaynor broke up the place and received critical acclaim. *Life* magazine said she started at the top and climbed even higher. The *Los Angeles Times* called her the nation's #1 female song-and-dance star and *The Hollywood Reporter* proclaimed her flawless and devastating.

Business was said to beat out the Vegas competitors Red Skelton, Joey Bishop, Martin & Lewis and even Sinatra. After Christmas and New Year's, when usually there was very little business, she was still a sell-out. She smashed all records at the hotel and more than 1000 customers were turned away nightly. She loved doing the act. Vegas crowds were different to those in Hot Springs. Here it wasn't considered rude to interrupt her numbers. These people just wanted to have a good time, and they had a ball with her.

Landsberg immediately wanted Gaynor for the next year and the year after; she ended up spending four years with the hotel. Thanks to her share of the profits and salary, Gaynor made a fortune that promised lifelong financial security. For the rest of the decade, Las Vegas remained her main professional playground. Audiences could always count on a show packed with singing, sex appeal and sensational costumes. Jack said that when she walked out on stage, you knew her whole heart and soul was in it. He had seen her work before 13,000 to 14,000 people and in front of 23 with 1100 seats empty, and the shows

6. Las Vegas

were identical. It was reported that more than 50,000 people came to see the shows.

Offstage she found fulfillment in her close marriage and her equally close relationship with her mother Pauline, who remained Gaynor's greatest champion. Mitzi had often thought of becoming a mother, and she and Jack had a lot of fun trying. But she had seen a lot of show business kids who had to travel, which was hard on them, and Gaynor didn't think she could make it work. Also, she felt too possessive towards Jack and didn't want to share him with anyone else. Her demanding work schedule meant that she was not destined to be a mother, so Gaynor channeled her energy into her work.

In February, Gaynor was to appear in the Casanova Room of the Deauville Hotel in Miami Beach. The Deauville was the sister hotel to the Flamingo. On March 21, it was reported that she was being considered to play the central character in a new stage musical about the Peace Corps. It had a book by Dr. Jack Weinstock and Willie Gilbert with a score by Mary Rodgers and lyrics by Martin Charnin. The producers were Robert Fryer and Lawrence Carr. Rehearsals were expected to begin in August with a Broadway opening in November. It was hoped that Morton DaCosta would direct.

Gaynor was reportedly considered for the role of Janet Walker in the Universal comedy *Bedtime Story* (1964), but Shirley Jones was cast instead. On July 24, it was announced that she would appear in the Universal comedy *Three on a Match*, to be directed by Michael Gordon. The color film, which came out as *For Love or Money*, was shot from August 7 to late September at Universal. The Larry Markes-Michael Morris screenplay focused on San Francisco attorney Deke Gentry (Kirk Douglas), hired to fix up the three daughters of heiress Chloe Brasher (Thelma Ritter) with suitable husbands. Second-billed Gaynor plays daughter Kate, a motivational researcher. She looks thinner and her hair by Larry Germain is full and worn in a flip.

The role sees Kate interact with a dog, play drunk, do some kissing, slap Deke, cry and dance with Sonny Smith (Gig Young) and Deke. The crying scene (perhaps Gaynor's best to date) allows Kate to transition to disbelief and anger at Deke's manipulation. Kate falls twice into the sea from a boat with Gaynor apparently assisted by a stunt double. The flattering costumes are by Jean Louis.

The film was released on August 7, 1963, with the taglines "What happens when a bachelor plays Matchmaker ... for 3 luscious sisters!!!"

and "He was hired to Mate them ... but not to Date them!!!" *Variety* wrote that Gaynor played vivaciously. Bosley Crowther in *The New York Times* said she played stylishly.

Gaynor agreed to teach Douglas "The Twist" after she observed that his attempt at dancing bore more resemblance to the "March of the Wooden Soldiers." The dance lesson came early in the production and was an icebreaker for the pair, who didn't really know each other. Douglas learned the dance on the spot. She felt that in the dance scene, Douglas was deft at handling comedic bits of dialogue by the sheer force of his amazing talent. Another icebreaking moment came when he wondered aloud about his motivation for crossing the room during a scene. Gaynor assured him his motivation was money and he got the joke. She was grateful to have the opportunity to make a film with him—even though it was a real dog.

This was to be her last film. She had the opportunity to do more at Universal, even one with Brando, which was presumably *Bedtime Story*. But Gaynor was now having more fun on stage and TV. Although Gaynor believed she was good in *Golden Girl* and *South Pacific* and danced very well in *Les Girls*, she felt that being a movie actress was a skill she didn't have. Also, there had never been any place for her in the movies. She had talent but no persona.

Coming from the stage as a smart aleck kid who knew everybody's part and lines and the staging, she was impatient. Filmmaking was a slow process after you had done a whole play in two and a half hours. The camera always seemed to be intruding on her, a voyeur over her shoulder. And Gaynor couldn't do the politics or be pushy. People who were pushy embarrassed her. Gaynor couldn't grab a producer at a cocktail party to demand a part or tell him she would do anything for it. You had to take Gaynor for what she was. Or look at her work because that is what Gaynor did. There was an element of unhappiness about not being more successful in films. But when she looked back at some of her performances, she was appalled by her acting.

Marilyn Monroe died on August 4. Sandra Shevey writes in *The Marilyn Scandal: Her True Life Revealed by Those Who Knew Her* that Gaynor wanted to attend the August 8 funeral. But Joe DiMaggio, who arranged the ceremony at the Westwood Village Memorial Park Cemetery, barred almost all Hollywood people, believing that if it wasn't for them, Monroe would still be alive.

It was reported on October 6 that New York's Americana Hotel

6. Las Vegas

Kirk Douglas (sitting on floor), Mitzi and director Michael Gordon on the set of *For Love or Money* (1963).

was negotiating for Gaynor to perform at its new nightclub, the Royal Box. On October 25, she attended the premiere of Ethel Merman's act at the Flamingo in Las Vegas. On November 3, it was reported that Gaynor was scheduled to return to the Casanova Room of the Deauville Hotel in Miami Beach in the winter. She reportedly made an appearance at L.A.'s Biltmore Hotel the week of February 10, 1964.

Gaynor was a guest on *The Ed Sullivan Show*'s February 16 episode, broadcast live from the stage of Miami Beach's Deauville Hotel. (One source claims that she actually performed at the convention hall.) She performed three numbers: singing and dancing Cole Porter's "It's Too Darn Hot" with chorus boys, singing "The More I See You" (music by Harry Warren and lyrics by Mack Gordon) and singing and dancing with the chorus boys a medley of blues numbers: "The Birth of the Blues" (music by Ray Henderson, lyrics by Buddy G. DeSylva and Lew Brown), "St. James Infirmary" (Irving Mills), "When the Saints Go Marching In" (music by James Milton Black, lyrics by Katharine E. Purvis), the traditional "Joshua Fit the Battle of Jericho" and a reprise of "When the Saints Go Marching In."

Being a live performance, Gaynor hits a few bum notes and we see her sweat. Her best number is perhaps "The More I See You." Sullivan said that the act was staged by Robert Sidney. Sidney wrote in his book *With Malice Towards Some: Tales from a Life Dancing with the Stars* that they simply duplicated the opening of her live show.

Sullivan also said that the greatest thrill for his other guests, the Beatles, was that Gaynor was going to be on the show. (According to Gaynor, children lined the streets to catch a glimpse of the Beatles. When Gaynor waved at the children, they didn't know who she was.) Gaynor commented that Sullivan had tried to get her on his show for ten years. Jack refused because he felt that Sullivan interrupted the entertainer's performances. So for the 1963 appearance, a deal was worked out that Gaynor would be given 13 minutes. In one interview, she claimed that Sullivan promised her eight minutes but the viewed footage shows her doing 13. Gaynor talked to the audience between "The More I See You" and the medley.

The medley's running time makes it more like the stage show performance that it is, rather than a performance designed for TV. "The More I See You" has Gaynor in a spotlight and alternates between medium shots and long shots. In the long shots, you can make out the band in the background.

There's a good reason why Sullivan had presumably never allowed an act to perform this long on his show before. It's too much for a TV audience to endure. What is tolerable on stage isn't necessarily tolerable on television. Even a seven-minute musical number in a feature film would be hard to accept, no matter how brilliant the execution.

After Gaynor danced on *Ed Sullivan*, the Catholic Church banned her act for being lascivious. This was due to Gaynor's sweating in the low-cut gown she wore to sing "The More I See You" and the blues medley. The response of the Catholic Church was especially hurtful as she was Catholic. Gaynor perspired because the room was packed with audience members and the air conditioning ducts were covered by lights—not to mention the Florida heat. No one seemed to mind how she repeatedly exposed her underpants when she swirled up the dress skirt dancing to "It's Too Darn Hot."

She was invited to have dinner with the Beatles at the hotel. The Beatles kissed her and asked for her autograph. Paul McCartney told her that they couldn't believe they were on the same show. Ultimately she felt it was a wonderful show. Gaynor never felt that the audience wanted her

6. Las Vegas

off so that the Beatles could come on (though that may have been true). She never again appeared on *Ed Sullivan* because Sullivan could never again promise her 13 minutes.

Robert Sidney reported that Gaynor and the chorus boys were to perform on a platform in the hotel ballroom. But the CBS technicians couldn't pipe the electric cables into the stage. It was agreed to do the first number on an improvised platform and then return to the theater for the regular show. The platform was half the size of the space she was accustomed to, but Gaynor and the boys managed it brilliantly.

Gaynor was part of two political fund-raising shows ("A Salute to Lyndon B. Johnson") sponsored by the Democratic National Committee. They were held at Washington's National Guard Armory on May 28 and in New York's Madison Square Garden on May 30. As part of the Salute entertainment directed by Richard Adler, Gaynor performed with chorus boys billed as "Her Gentlemen." She and Jack were later invited to a State Dinner at the White House in honor of German Chancellor Ludwig Erhard and lunched with the president's family during her engagement at Washington, D.C.'s Carter Barron Amphitheater.

In June 27, Gaynor and Jack attended the wedding of Ethel Merman and Ernest Borgnine in a civil ceremony at the bridegroom's home. The reception was held at Chasen's Restaurant. In November, they attended the opening night of Liza Minnelli at the Cocoanut Grove.

A 1965 souvenir program for "Mitzi Gaynor and Company" at the Melodyland Theatre in Anaheim, California, has her performing with the Clara Ward Singers and the Four Fellows. The Fellows are listed as Michael Gray, Alton Ruff, Bud Vest and Jimmy Weiss. The show was produced and directed by Robert Sidney, with choreography by Jack Baker, costumes by Robert Carlton and hair by Tom Carlino. It included "Too Darn Hot" and the *Ed Sullivan Show* blues medley. There were also The Hollywood Cavalcade characters plus "Honey Bun" and "Wonderful Guy" from *South Pacific* from Gaynor's Vegas act. New material included comedy dialogue by Bruce Howard, "I'm All Smiles" by Michael Leonard and Herbert Martin, "A Gospel Meetin'" which had a song with the Clara Ward Singers, and a solo "Bossa Nova" medley.

In the program notes, she reported on recently doing a one-nighter to 6000 people at the Concord Hotel in the Catskills. The audience was mostly sophisticated New Yorkers who had seen everything, so Gaynor really had to work at reaching them. Other recent shows were in Washington and Detroit. This new kind of audience expected more careful production, technical excellence, and a longer, polished, professional show. So she tried a little harder for them and sometimes they loved her back.

Gaynor was a guest on TV's *Danny Thomas Special: My Home Town* (February 6, 1966), written by Milt Rosen, directed by Alan Handley and filmed on the MGM backlot. She performed two numbers: singing and dancing "The Boy from Ipanema" (a variation of the song "The Girl from Ipanema," music by Antônio Carlos Jobim and lyrics by Norman Gimbel) and duetting with Jim Nabors on "Only a Rose" (music by Rudolf Friml, lyrics by Brian Hooker and William H. Post). Gaynor also joined Thomas and Nabors in costume, spoofing old war, pirate, and romantic pictures. Their targets included the old Jeanette MacDonald-Nelson Eddy type of movie musical.

Like Ed Sullivan, Danny Thomas had been keeping after Jack about having Mitzi on his show. She met with the show's costume designer Ray Aghayan and clicked with him; according to Gaynor, he was Persian and fun and gorgeous.

Gaynor was considered for the part of Guenevere in the film of the Broadway musical *Camelot* (1967) but Vanessa Redgrave was cast instead. Another part for which she was considered: burlesque performer Rachel Schpitendavel in the United Artists comedy *The Night They Raided Minsky's* (1968). Britt Ekland was cast instead.

On September 21, 1966, Gaynor moved from the Flamingo to the Riviera, where she stayed for six years. It was here that her long association with Bob Mackie began. Aghayan was unavailable for the show so he sent Mackie in his place. She was at rehearsal in her leotard and matching scarf and four-inch heels when there was a knock on the door. This little blonde head appeared and there was a man with a broken voice who Gaynor assumed wanted her autograph. He introduced himself as Bob Mackie and she commented that his voice hadn't changed yet and invited him in.

Mackie said that Gaynor discovered him but she would say Mackie discovered *her*, the real her. He was bright, terribly chic very fashion-conscious, and with a tremendous sense of humor. Mackie said Gaynor was vibrant, bubbly, funny and fantastic. She wanted to update her costumes and move into the 1960s, Gaynor keeping her career on track despite the huge changes in popular culture.

6. Las Vegas

Classic floor-length gowns and cocktail dresses were replaced with miniskirts, go-go boots and the latest in mod fashion. Mackie said she loved opulence and color. Her favorite was pink. Gaynor would never wear anything slightly muted like gray or beige without it being beaded or bejeweled. Mackie saw that her act could have anywhere from 10 to 20 costume changes in an hour. Everything had to make audience members smile because that's what she was all about.

The designer made everything she wore on stage or on television specials from then on. His clothes were so good that she could do eight shows a week on stage for five years in them. One thing Gaynor taught him was something she learned from Ginger Rogers: When an entertainer goes in for a fitting, she should not stand like a mannequin. You had to move around and stretch and bend over, as you would do in performance, so that if something popped, you could mend it.

On April 10, Gaynor performed at *The 39th Annual Academy Awards*, held at the Santa Monica Civic Auditorium. With four Ernie Flatt Dancers, she sang and danced "Georgy Girl" (music by Tom Springfield, lyrics by Jim Dale), a Best Song nominee. She begins as a schoolgirl in a shapeless orange smock with a polka-dot Breton hat over a pig-tailed wig, bow tie and oversized horn-rimmed glasses. Gaynor then ripped off the outfit to reveal a Mackie hot pink leotard festooned with a blazing orange sequined fringe. The choreographer was Ernie Flatt. The number reportedly got the longest ovation in Oscar history.

When Gaynor was offered the chance to do "Georgy Girl," neither she nor Jack knew what "Georgy Girl" was, because they hadn't seen the recent film of that title. At the dress rehearsal, her costume wasn't ready so she wore a mock-up over an old pair of tights and dance shoes. The show's producer Joe Pasternak saw her after the rehearsal and told the sweaty Gaynor that she looked wonderful. He wanted to know if she was going to wear a costume for the performance and Gaynor said of course she would. She couldn't believe that a man with his experience would ask such a question.

Gaynor was allowed her own piano player, guitarist and drummer all playing on the set. She and the dancers froze at the end of the number as the audience stood and applauded. As she stood with her hands raised, through her teeth she asked when they could break. Finally she took it upon herself to break and take a bow. She said it was the most thrilling night of her life.

Gaynor standing around boys of the St. Thomas Church Choir in *The Kraft Music Hall* TV presentation "Mitzi Gaynor Christmas Show."

6. Las Vegas

Gaynor claims that she appeared on the May 11 episode of the musical TV series *Las Vegas* with Bill Dana. This cannot be confirmed.

Gaynor's stage show was performed at the South Shore Room Theatre Restaurant at Harrah's Lake Tahoe for three weeks starting on August 16, 1967. The format had been changed earlier in the year to be different to previous seasons offered in Vegas and Harrah's. Now it included a talented young ventriloquist, musicians and others. She boasted that three weeks at Harrah's was like a small vacation. She found the audiences to be fabulous, as was Bill Harrah.

After the run, she and Jack planned a well-earned vacation. Gaynor envisioned a long ocean trip, perhaps to the Orient. But since Jack preferred planes, they might compromise with half-flying and half-sailing. On October 19 at the New York Public Library, she drew the winning ticket for the monthly state lottery. On December 7, she lit the Christmas tree in Rockefeller Center.

Frank Vlastnik and Laura Ross write in their book *The Art of Bob Mackie* that after Gaynor's Academy Awards performance, NBC approached her about doing a TV special. Up until this time, Gaynor had chosen to keep her TV dates infrequent. Gaynor didn't like being a guest shot performer because you didn't get enough to do when you were on someone else's show. She liked to sit down and stay awhile. Gaynor had been offered many TV series but always turned them down.

NBC decided to test out ratings by having her appear in an episode of *The Kraft Music Hall*, "Mitzi Gaynor Christmas Show," shot at the NBC in New York and broadcast on December 20. The director was Dwight Hemion, the choreographer Peter Gennaro. She sang a medley with chorus of "We Need a Little Christmas" (by Jerry Herman); the traditional "Deck the Halls" (lyrics by Thomas Oliphant), sung with Cyril Ritchard and Tony Tanner; "The Christmas Song" (by Robert Wells and Mel Tormé), sung with Ed McMahon; a reprise of "We Need a Little Christmas"; a medley of carols by Alfred Burt, sung with the St. Thomas Church Choir; dancing "White Christmas" as a toy soldier with chorus boy soldiers; and a medley of "I Believe in You" (by Frank Loesser) and "Have Yourself a Merry Little Christmas" (by Hugh Martin and Ralph Blaine), sung with Ed McMahon. Gaynor and McMahon also read comic letters to Santa. (She said the fun of the show was being with McMahon, who was determined to sing. While not a great singer his performance was passable.)

Other sources indicate that Gaynor as the toy soldier also danced "Parade of the Wooden Soldiers" (by Leon Jessel) with the chorus boy soldiers. Other numbers included "I Dig Rock'n'Roll Music" (by Paul Stookey, James Mason and Dave Dixon) with Gaynor dressed as Raggedy Ann and chorus boys as Raggedy Andys, "I Know a Place" (by Tony Hatch), with carolers singing a medley of the traditional "God Rest Ye Merry Gentlemen" and "It Came Upon a Midnight Clear" (music by Richard Storrs Willis, lyrics by Edmund Sears), "Hark the Herald Angels Sing" (music by Felix Mendelssohn, lyrics by Charles Wesley and George Whitefield) and "Our Town," and a jazz number. In addition, there was a skit with Cyril Ritchard and Tony Tanner about Scrooge and Bob Cratchit, a rendition of "A Wonderful Day Like Today" (by Leslie Bricusse and Anthony Newley) and more.

Neil Genzlinger in *The New York Times* noted that Gaynor infused the show with an energy that contrasted noticeably with specials headlined by bigger stars who seemed to sleepwalk through them.

7

Mitzi

On June 5, NBC announced a new Gaynor special. Executive produced by Jack, *Mitzi* was shot at the NBC Studios in Hollywood in July and broadcast on October 14. It was written by Larry Hovis and Ann Edler and produced and directed by Bob Henry. Costumes were by Bob Mackie, hair by Tom Carlino and choreography by Peter Gennaro. Gaynor performs seven numbers: dancing with singing and dancing chorus boys in "Everybody Loves My Baby" (music by Spencer Williams, lyrics by Jack Palmer); singing "Laura" (music by David Raksin, lyrics by Johnny Mercer) accompanied by chorus boys; singing "Gentle on My Mind" (by John Hartford), singing and dancing a hillbilly medley of "Flowers on the Wall" (Lew DeWitt), "Yakety Sax" (James Q. "Spider" Rich, Boots Randolph) and "Entrance of the Gladiators" op. 68 (Julius Fučík) accompanied by dancing chorus boys; singing "Love Is Blue" (music by André Popp, lyrics by Bryan Blackbur), accompanied by an unseen chorus; dancing "Pretty for Me" (sung by an unseen chorus) with chorus boys; and dancing with chorus boys in "Long Ago (and Far Away)" (music by Jerome Kern, lyrics by Ira Gershwin) to an unseen chorus.

The latter number is a spoof of the title song danced by Rita Hayworth in the film *Cover Girl* (1944). It was part of a series of spoofs of late-night movies. The others include Gaynor playing Rosalind Russell from *His Girl Friday* in "The Lady" and Doris Day in "Pillow Fight" as a spoof of *Pillow Talk*. The idea of Day repeatedly changing her clothes in the skit is a funny one and achieved via editing. The show also features Gaynor as Oola May Purdue from West Virginia, a Southern-accented hillbilly who dances and sings three of the musical numbers.

There is also a location segment filmed by John Urie with makeup-free, flat-haired Gaynor as a lonely, baseball cap–wearing girl

Gaynor in her 1968 TV special *Mitzi*.

7. Mitzi

known as The Kid. She delivers a monologue to-camera and in voice-over and sings "Happiness" by David Benoit with an unseen whistler and then orchestra. This segment is perhaps the most radical of the show but director Urie uses too many camera tricks which distract from the performance. He has superimposed images from two camera angles, our view of Gaynor obstructed by trees and a fence, the camera out of focus, sun flares, extreme long shots and extreme closeups. Gaynor was brave to appear without makeup. The segment is overlong at six minutes.

The show's director Bob Henry uses an inverted image of Gaynor (her reflection on a polished floor) under the opening credits. He has some fast edits of the set blocks and of Gaynor in the beginning of "Everybody Loves My Baby." However for this number, the hillbilly medley, "Pretty for Me" and "Long Ago (and Far Away)," Henry alternates between medium and long shots for the dancing coverage, which is frustrating when Gaynor's feet are cut off in medium shots. "Long Ago (and Far Away)" also has superimposed images, and with a running time of four minutes is too long. The original number in *Cover Girl* only runs for two minutes, which demonstrates how bloated the parody is.

The alternate medium, longer shots, closeups and different camera angles are less distracting in a singing performance like "Gentle on My Mind." That number even has Gaynor walk and the camera stays with her in a medium shot. "Love Is Blue" uses superimposed images and set trees and plastic windows that sometimes block our view of her.

The writers supply some amusing self-referential touches. The opening of the show has The Kid deface portraits of Gaynor; then she appears in a glamorous gown and a mustache. Gaynor presents a kit bag which produces canned applause, which is ironic given the canned laughter on the soundtrack. Oola May comments on Gaynor's hanging wardrobe as being that of a bad girl and asks which of the chorus boys she meets is Mitzi Gaynor. She also cleans dirt from the camera lens.

Gaynor reported that when shooting "Love Is Blue" she saw Bob Mackie on set watching her with a screwed-up face, as if he was wondering what she was doing. Her beige beaded evening gown was so tight, Gaynor could hardly breathe and her performance was channeling Jean Cocteau's *La Belle et la Bête*. She later admitted it was so dramatic that it was unintentionally funny. (In my opinion, Gaynor was not as over-dramatic as she feared.)

The Kid originated in the Vegas act and was inspired by Gaynor's childhood, which was lonely before she began to dance. Mackie said that upon first seeing Gaynor without makeup, he didn't recognize her. The segment was shot in a schoolyard.

Gaynor reported that Larry Hovis and Ann Edler had devised material for her stage show, which is why they were hired for the special. The writers knew her so well that the dialogue practically wrote itself. She was particularly pleased with the late-night movie spoofs, feeling they were inventive and exciting.

Frank Vlastnik and Laura Ross write in their book on Bob Mackie that the success of the show made Gaynor the most glamorous dancing variety star on TV for the next decade.

Mackie had a special feeling about the show because it was his first with a star. He felt it had everything a show should have: glamor and fun. It was the one he was most nostalgic about and his favorite of the ones he did with Gaynor.

NBC called it "The Night Belongs to Mitzi" because she was also a guest on *The Bob Hope Special* and that night's episode of *Rowan & Martin's Laugh-In*. For Hope, Gaynor came on like Betty Grable with big sculptured hair curls, a Hawaiian skirt and high-heeled wedgies with ankle straps. She did a hula dance and when he asked, "Is it Hawaii or Havaii?" she replied, "Havaii." Hope thanked her and Gaynor said, "You're velcome." He then told the audience that her show could be seen later that night. Her *Laugh-In* skit was set at a fashion show-cocktail party.

Mitzi was a critical and ratings smash with 33 million viewers. CBS was eager for her to return for an annual special in between Gaynor's stage engagements. It was said the shows always tested her imagination and she would accept any challenge. Once committing herself, Gaynor worked tirelessly. Jack had negotiated a cash windfall and the exposure gave her the ability to book the next year's touring. Sometimes she would lift a segment honed on the road in her nightclub act and put it into the next TV show—and sometimes it was the other way around. She made her money from Vegas and touring her act, including the summer tent circuit and, later, large performing arts centers. These venues certainly paid her more than doing a Broadway show or TV guest spots.

During her 1969 vacation in Hawaii, Gaynor had the idea for her next TV special. When she and Jack was sunning themselves on

7. Mitzi

Waikiki Beach, the song "Let Go" came on the radio. The pair looked at each and nodded, both knowing this was the theme and the feeling they wanted. The show was taped in July at the same time as the moon landing. Gaynor cried at the moment of touchdown.

Mitzi's 2nd Special was broadcast on October 13, 1969, again written by Larry Hovis and Ann Edler. Some of the chorus boys are credited as The Four Fellows: Alton Ruff, Randy Doney, Bart Carroll and Michael Gray. The new choreographer was Danny Daniels. Jack Bean and Bob Mackie appear in the show, under the end credits. Mitzi performed four numbers: singing and dancing "Let Go" (by Norman Gimbel, Baden Powell and Vinicius De Moraes), accompanied by chorus boys; singing and dancing "Poor Papa (He's Got Nuthin' At All)" (music by Harry Woods, lyrics by Billy Rose), performed with chorus boys; singing and dancing a medley of "Spinning Wheel" (David Clayton-Thomas), "Walk on By" (music by Burt Bacharach, lyrics by Hal David), "What'll I Do" (Irving Berlin), "Son of a Preacher Man" (Ronnie Wilkins, John Hurley), accompanied by an unseen chorus; and singing and dancing a gypsy song and "Those Were the Days" (Boris Fomin, Gene Raskin) with the boys' chorus.

In a skit parody of *Gone with the Wind*, entitled "Hello Charlotte," Gaynor vocalizes to "Hello, Dolly!" (by Jerry Herman); imitates Ethel Merman singing "The Guy That I Marry," a variation on Irving Berlin's "The Girl That I Marry"; sings "The Hula Hoop Song" (Donna Kohler, Carl Maduri), "Ol' Man River" (music by Jerome Kern, lyrics by Oscar Hammerstein II) and "You Are My Sunshine" (Jimmie Davis, Charles Mitchell). The Kid returns for a monologue and dance recital performance where she sings "Away in a Manger" (William J. Kirkpatrick, James Ramsey Murray) and the Joyce Kilmer poem "Trees." Gaynor also has linking monologues about the show's theme of "Let Go," the set paintings and chair, her childhood as a dancer, being Hungarian, cleaning and cooking. In these monologues, Gaynor does funny French and Hungarian accents.

This special features the best musical numbers in Gaynor's TV specials to date in terms of director coverage. The "Spinning Wheel" medley has Gaynor's best singing, showing her ability to enliven cover songs, even when she is occasionally over-dramatic. Director Richard Dunlap alternates between long and medium shots, and uses psychedelic lighting. Gaynor begins "What'll I Do" in long shot with her back to the camera.

For "Let Go," where she wears a Mackie nude illusion fringed dress, Dunlap uses zooms among the long shots of the dancing. In "Poor Papa (He's Got Nuthin' At All)," Gaynor's sailor drag recalls "A Sailor's Not a Sailor ('Till a Sailor's Been Tattooed)" from *There's No Business Like Show Business* and she sings like Ethel Merman. Dunlap alternates between medium and long shots, the long shots featuring most of the dancing coverage. The directorial choice to have these two numbers back to back is a sign of excess, a notion pointed out by Gaynor in her first monologue where she talks about having a rest period. Again on the same date, Gaynor was seen first on *The Bob Hope Special* and *Rowan & Martin's Laugh-In*.

In the "Hello Charlotte" skit, Gaynor has three changes of costume and Ross Martin imitates Clark Gable and sings like Louis Armstrong and Ezio Pinza. With a running time of ten minutes, it overstays its welcome. Gaynor said they had a censor problem with using *Gone with the Wind*'s "I don't give a damn" line because you could not say *damn* on TV.

Dunlap uses a water optical effect and psychedelic lights for "You Are My Sunshine."

The Kid opens the show, Gaynor wearing eye makeup and lipstick. The Kid walks onto the set and finds a crate with the show's credits on it. She imitates the pose Gaynor assumes in a stuck-on photograph and then the crate opens to reveal a cameraman inside. The Kid's return is foreshadowed by some lines heard during a Gaynor bridging monologue. When she appears for the recital skit,

Gaynor and chorus boys in *Mitzi's 2nd Special* (1969).

7. Mitzi

the Kid now wears no makeup. The skit allows us to see Gaynor dance on-point, but it's undermined by canned laughter and its excessive running time. When the Kid asks us to close our eyes, the screen goes black. The special won the Emmy for Outstanding Achievement in Art Direction or Scenic Design: For a Variety Single Program.

Interviewed at the time, Gaynor said her legs were the foundation of her career. Dance training gave you confidence and poise, making you graceful and secure in the way you moved, which was important to actors and singers. The confidence from dancing also made Gaynor wear clothes well and she was able to use clothes in her routines to set the desired mood.

Gaynor wanted to do more films. She was still doing nightclubs which, according to Gaynor, was the only place you could break in new material. She liked to go to Lake Tahoe or Las Vegas where there was a good cross section of people in her audiences.

On July 6, 1970, Gaynor played a week at the O'Keefe Centre in Toronto, Canada. On July 16, she began a singing engagement at New York's Plaza Hotel. She played the Westbury Music Fair in New York from August 11 to 16, 1970.

Gaynor was a guest on CBS's *The Merv Griffin Show* on December 10. The episode was a tribute to producer Ross Hunter; Gaynor's connection with Hunter was that she was to star in his new film *Hollywood, Hollywood*, about movies and movie stars of the 1930s, with Lucille Ball and Carol Burnett. The film was never made. Perhaps because of its cancellation, Gaynor now had no desire to do films. The TV specials were her movies. She loved TV because it was fast, the production of a special taking two weeks. (Gaynor later said that for her specials, dance rehearsal alone took two to three weeks.) Endlessly waiting around on movie sets was not something she liked.

In 1970, Gaynor became the first distaff performer awarded the Nevada Governor's Trophy in recognition of her outstanding contribution to Nevada's fame as the entertainment mecca of the world. On June 13, 1971, she was part of the Frank Sinatra Retirement Concert held at the Ahmanson Theater in L.A.'s Dorothy Chandler Pavilion. It was a benefit for the Motion Picture and Television Relief Fund. She reportedly sang and danced with four chorus boys.

She was a guest on the TV special *Perry Como's Winter Show*, shot at the NBC studios in Hollywood and broadcast on December 9. It had multiple writers and was directed by Marty Pasetta. Costumed by

Bob Mackie, Gaynor performed a number with Como and Art Carney. The show had started shooting in October but it was suspended when Como stepped on a fake snowflake and broke his leg. Thereafter, the cast had to work fast and shoot the whole thing in one day. She called Como "El Supremo" and said he was a charming and fun person. She wanted to have him in one of her next specials, and Lucille Ball in another. Neither of these castings would happen.

Gaynor's nightclub act was seen in Reno, Harrah's again in Lake Tahoe, and then Honolulu. In Hawaii, Gaynor renewed her friendship with Dr. and Mrs. Kenneth Fuji. After finishing her act in Miami, she intended to go on a long vacation—maybe Copenhagen, Mexico or the Orient. It was said Gaynor now played three to four months on the road earning $80,000 a week, and devoted the rest of the year to performing her next act.

On May 19, Gaynor was on *The Tonight Show Starring Johnny Carson,* singing "Poor Papa." She reported wearing a tiny gold sailor's outfit with four-inch heels. When Gaynor exited, Carson said that she was really built. But Ed McMahon's addition ("Like a—") was cut from the broadcast.

Gaynor was a presenter at *Cavalcade of Champions,* an NBC-TV sports broadcast on March 27.

8

Mitzi ... The First Time

Her next television special *Mitzi ... The First Time* (broadcast on March 28) was written by Jerry Mayer and Stanley Ralph Ross, with special musical material by Dick De Benedictis and Bill Dyer. The choreographer was Robert Sidney. She sings part of "The First Time Ever I Saw Your Face" (by Ewan MacColl); sings "Alice Blue Gown" (Joseph McCarthy and Harry Tierney) with an unseen chorus; sings "A First Time" (De Benedictis and Dyer) and "Them There Eyes" (Maceo Pinkard, Doris Tauber and William Tracey) with Dan Dailey, Ken Berry and Mike Connors; sings and dances in the Funhouse "The First Dance" (De Benedictis and Dyer), "I'm All Smiles" (Michael Leonard and Herbert Martin) with Berry and accompanied by an unseen chorus, sings "Yadda Yadda" (Dore Previn) with Berry, and sings and dances "When I'm Sixty-Four" (John Lennon and Paul McCartney) with Berry; sings and dances with Dailey a medley of "It Had to Be You" (music by Isham Jones, lyrics by Gus Kahn) and "You Are My Lucky Star" (music by Nacio Herb Brown, lyrics by Arthur Freed); dances to "Take Me Out to the Ballgame" (Jack Norworth and Albert Von Tilzer); sings and dances with Dailey, Berry and Connors "A Sailor's Not a Sailor ('Til a Sailor's Been Tattooed)" (Irving Berlin); sings and dances "Limehouse Blues" (music by Philip Braham, lyrics by Douglas Furber), sings "Chic Soap" (De Benedictis and Dyer) with Dailey, Berry and Connors; and sings the full version of "The First Time Ever I Saw Your Face."

This time, the only number that is too long is the full version of "The First Time Ever I Saw Your Face." A 13-minute funhouse location sequence incorporates a "first time" theme with segments on the First Dance, the First Night of the Wedding and the First News of the Grandchild. There is also a ten-minute makeup table bridge where Gaynor, Dailey, Berry and Connors prepare to shoot the Chic Soap television commercial. They reminisce about the First Time They Got Hooked on Show Business, which allows for four numbers. The "first time" theme is continued with Gaynor's "First Fan Letter," which leads to two songs performed with Dailey.

This show is different for Gaynor in that it gives solo performing time to some of the guests. As part of the makeup table segment, Connors recites and sings "Watching Scotty Grow" by Mac Davis, and he and Berry sing "You Can Do It" by De Benedictis and Dyer. Director John Moffitt covers Connors' solo performance in profile shots, superimposed images and long closeups. The latter seems particularly perverse considering that Connors is not much of a singer.

The Kid character, now with curly hair and Gaynor's makeup and wearing a dress, appears in the funhouse bridge and in "The First Dance," and dances with Berry. This segment is in black-and-white, with postcard-type images for transition before and after.

Gaynor is perhaps best in "A Sailor's Not a Sailor ('Til a Sailor's Been Tattooed)" from *There's No Business Like Show Business*. In sailor drag, she performs with Dailey, Berry and Connors. Moffitt covers the dancing mostly in long shots though at one point there is an odd backstage point-of-view shot.

Gaynor's face looks a little heavier perhaps due to a new sculptured hairdo. But worse is that her solos are undercut by Moffitt. "Alice Blue Gown" has alternate medium and long shots for the dancing but too many camera angles. It ends on a freeze frame, which is an interesting touch. Her dance to "Take Me Out to the Ballgame" is done in front of a baseball scoreboard; she momentarily goes into the board and becomes an animated figure. Director Moffitt alternates between medium and long shots for the dancing and has some zoom-ins and -outs.

"Limehouse Blues" has another spectacular Mackie nude illusion outfit with Gaynor in a cage. Moffitt has the glitter of the costume and the cage give camera reflective flares. However he uses multiple superimpositions for her dance. This is perhaps done to hide the split in the dress of the costume that seems to expose Gaynor's crotch. Her full version of "The First Time Ever I Saw Your Face" is performed over-dramatically. Moffitt uses superimpositions and ends on three images of the singer.

Moffitt also zooms in and out of long shots for "Yadda Yadda," "I'm All Smiles" and the "It Had to Be You" medley. Mitzi Gerber in pigtails and nightgown changes to Gaynor in a ballgown and then back again

8. Mitzi ... The First Time

at the end. Other optical effects are the superimposed eyes of Dailey, Berry and Connors, seen when she sings "Them There Eyes"; a frosted camera for "I'm All Smiles"; split screen for "When I'm Sixty-Four," and bubbles for the Chic Soap commercial.

Gaynor changes from a virgin in a wedding gown to a sexually demanding vamp in a negligee for "Yadda Yadda." There is wit in Gaynor's opening monologue where she says the show will be simple, and we see her in a montage of eight outrageous Mackie glamor outfits. Within this montage, there is a superimposed shot of Gaynor when she says the show will have no gimmicks. There is less canned laughter than in the previous specials.

Gaynor performed at Starlight '73 in Swope Park, Kansas City, Missouri, from August 6 to 12. It included "It Had to Be You" and "Those Were the Days" from her previous TV specials, and "You Are the Sunshine of My Life" and "Mitzi's Tribute to the Housewife," two numbers that were included in her new special. In September and October, she appeared at Harrah's Headliner Room in Reno as Mitzi Gaynor with the Big Surprise. She headlined the opening of the Tropicana Hotel's Superstar Theatre in Las Vegas on October 5.

Her next special, *Mitzi ... A Tribute to the American Housewife*, was broadcast on CBS on February 4, 1974. It was written by Jerry Mayer and Charlotte Brown, with special musical material by Dick De Benedictis and Bill Dyer. Tony Charmoli choreographed and directed. Jack Bean again appears in this show. Gaynor performs eight numbers: singing "Married" (by Fred Ebb and John Kander); moving in background while Ted Knight, Jerry Orbach and Cliff Norton sing "The Girl That I Marry" (Irving Berlin), then sang in a medley with "I'm a Woman" (Jerry Leiber and Mike Stoller) with Jane Withers and Suzanne Pleshette; dancing with chorus boys to "Dreams of the Everyday Housewife" (Chris Gantry), sung by Orbach; singing a medley of "And I Can Cook Too" (music by Leonard Bernstein, lyrics by Betty Comden and Adolph Green) and multiple other songs; singing a song about needling (De Benedictis and Dyer) with Withers and Pleshette; singing and dancing "I'd Do Anything" (Lionel Bart) with Knight; dancing at the PTA bazaar rehearsal, leading to her dancing to "Rhapsody in Blue" (George Gershwin); singing "The Little Things You Do Together" with the whole cast, and singing a medley of "Singin' in the Rain" (music by Nacio Herb Brown, lyrics by Arthur Freed) and "You Are the Sunshine of My Life" (Stevie Wonder).

Gaynor also appears is skits. In one of them, she, Winters and Pleshette are women at a hairdressers (Ted Knight), who do needlepoint under the dryers. The women have barbed dialogue and sing a song about needling. The skit has some funny lines and Gaynor smiles at Pleshette's "I wouldn't know what to do with a broom if you gave it to me."

In a skit with Knight and Norton, Gaynor plays an unappreciated housewife. Gaynor has a funny reaction to Knight calling her his maid. She and Knight also perform "I'd Do Anything." Another skit is set at the first annual Housewife of the Year Awards. Here Gaynor is seen in the audience with Winters, Pleshette (and extras), laughing at Knight singing "Mrs. American Housewife." She plays Nancy Neat, winner of the Ozzie & Harriet Good Housekeeping Award for Fastidious Cleanliness Indoors and Outdoors. Gaynor is funny in her acceptance speech. The final skit is a party scene in which Gaynor has a funny reaction to Norton (she assumes he is making a pass but he is actually more interested in her dress).

The show also has monologues by Gaynor, Knight (about his wife's use of the fridge, Pleshette (about her son) and Orbach (about his wife at parties). The special gives Pleshette a solo song, "Happiness," that Gaynor had sung as The Kid in *Mitzi*.

Director Charmoli uses superimpositions as Orbach sings "Dreams of the Everyday Housewife," in the "Singin' in the Rain"–"You Are the Sunshine of My Life" medley, and during "Rhapsody in Blue." The latter number has a wind machine, freeze frame, slow motion, duplicate and triplicate mirror images, Gaynor lying on a flying piano or a flying camera moving around the piano, and a reverse motion shot of the parachute around Gaynor as a coat. In "The Girl That I Marry," Charmoli has Gaynor, Withers and Pleshette breaking through a photograph of the cast. The number "And I Can Cook Too" came from Gaynor's stage show.

Howard Thompson in *The New York Times* wrote that Gaynor solo dances were expert and her straightforward rendition of "You Are the Sunshine of My Life" beautiful. The special won an Emmy for Outstanding Achievement in Choreography and was nominated for Best Directing in Comedy-Variety, Variety or Music and Outstanding Achievement in Lighting Direction.

Charmoli said that Gaynor was a star and didn't look like anyone else. But he thought the idea of a glamorous thing like her as a

8. Mitzi ... The First Time

(From left) Suzanne Pleshette, Gaynor and Jane Withers in *Mitzi ... A Tribute to the American Housewife* (1974).

housewife was pretty dull so he wanted to fluff it up. Gaynor felt that Charmoli was someone who knew all the sides of her. She considered him a true artist. He wanted to make a new Mitzi Gaynor and she was happy to do it. Mackie reported that Charmoli's enthusiasm and spirit were important to her since Gaynor needed to have a positive spirit on the set. Charmoli was especially interested in the "Rhapsody in Blue" number having a big-screen dimension and not be a typical television number. This led him to consult editors to learn what new techniques were available.

On February 28, Gaynor attended a pre–Grammy party for "Tie a Yellow Ribbon Round the Ole Oak Tree" songwriters Irwin Levine and L. Russell Brown at the Beverly Hills Hotel.

In 1971, Gaynor participated in advertising for Akai tape recorders and decks. The ad tagline was "Music is my business. That's why I own AKAI." On August 6, it was reported that Gaynor's relationship with Akai had soured. She complained that the company had failed to give her $13,000 in stereo equipment in return for her endorsement. Gaynor sued for $24 million. Damages specified in the suit included alleged loss of reputation, unauthorized use of photographs and possible business loss.

She was back at Harrah's in Reno through October 2. Gaynor was a presenter at *The 1974 Annual Las Vegas Entertainment Awards*, held at Caesar's Palace on November 20 and broadcast on NBC.

In 1974, Gaynor appeared at the Toledo Masonic Auditorium as part of Ken Shaw's Summer Star Theatre in Atlanta. It was reported on January 6, 1975, that Sakowitz of Houston, a store that specialized in hard-to-find goodies for Beautiful People, was selling Gaynor's Lessons in Dancing for $10,600. ("Lessons in Dancing" was a Christmas shopping gift offered by Gaynor for those customers of artistic bent. Peter Duchin offered "Lessons on Piano" for $3,750.) On March 21, she was back on *The Tonight Show*, this time performing "Four or Five Times" (by Byron Gay and Marco H. Hellman) with Jack Albertson.

Her next television special, CBS's *Mitzi and 100 Guys*, was broadcast on March 24. The show was written by Jerry Mayer with special musical material by Dick De Benedictis and Bill Dyer. The guest stars included the Million Dollar Chorus; 36 of them were male TV stars, the other 64 from the USC Trojan Marching Band.

Gaynor's face looks thinner here, with her hair worn off her forehead and less sculptured. Her false spider eyelashes are perhaps too

8. Mitzi ... The First Time

much. She performs in seven numbers: singing and dancing "I've Got the Music in Me" (by Bias Boshell) with singing and dancing chorus boys and her male guest stars; singing "Life Is a Rock (But the Radio Rolled Me)" (music by Paul DiFranco, lyrics by Norman Dolph) with Michael Landon; singing and dancing a medley of "Oh My My," "Boogie Down," "Keep on Truckin'," "Stop That You Stole My Heart" and "Got to Get You Into My Life"; singing "Always" (Irving Berlin) with posing musclemen; singing and dancing "It's De-Lovely" (Cole Porter) with Landon and "We've Got Us" (Benedictis and Dyer) with Landon and Jack Albertson; dancing to "Waiting for the Robert E. Lee" (L. Wolfe Gilbert and Lewis F. Muir) with the chorus boys and the USC Trojan Marching Band; and singing the medley of "Singin' in the Rain" and "You Are the Sunshine of My Life."

Two musical numbers have comic elements: "Stop That You Stole My Heart" (the male chorus repeats what Gaynor sings) and "It's De-Lovely" (Landon repeatedly falls into the set). The latter is paid off at the end of "We've Got Us" when she and Albertson fall out of frame though we don't see where they go. Gaynor has one monologue and a scream as a bridge, but otherwise the musical numbers are back to back. Albertson gets a solo singing "Mandy" by Scott English and Richard Kerr.

In "Waiting for the Robert E. Lee," director-choreographer Charmoli uses negative colors, triple mirrored images, superimpositions, slow motion, frosted camera edges and freeze frames. "I've Got the Music in Me," which runs under the opening credits, runs seven minutes. This is perhaps necessary: Charmoli has to cover all the male guest stars (who take turns walking down stairs in groups) and the chorus boys. Charmoli also uses superimpositions for the medley of "Singin' in the Rain" and "You Are the Sunshine of My Life." In the "Life Is a Rock (But the Radio Rolled Me)," the closeups are unflattering to Gaynor. In addition, from the eyelines of both Gaynor and Brandon, they appear to be reading the lyrics from an off-screen source. Given how complicated the lyrics are, that is understandable.

The 36 male television stars are under-used, seen only in "I've Got the Music in Me" at the beginning and at the end of the show when reprised by the chorus. When Gaynor kisses multiple guys on the mouth in succession, we fear for her hygiene. The special won the Emmy for Outstanding Achievement in Lighting Direction and was nominated for Outstanding Achievement in Technical Direction and Electronic Camerawork.

Gaynor in *Mitzi and 100 Guys* (1975).

8. Mitzi ... The First Time

It was reported that Gaynor and her 100 guys donated their fees to the Motion Picture and Television Relief Fund. She said *100 Guys* was Charmoli's idea. Some stars declined the offer to appear; Telly Savalas said yes but then became unavailable; Rowan and Martin were on vacation. Gaynor's pink and purple dress (by Bob Mackie) for "I've Got the Music in Me" had see-through lace at the bust and got the attention of the Guys as well as the sponsors.

In August, Gaynor appeared at the South Shore Music Centre in Cohasset, Massachusetts. On September 17, she was back at the Westbury Music Fair, and a return to Harrah's in Lake Tahoe. On March 12, Gaynor attended "The Costume Council of the Los Angeles County Museum of Art Presents Showtime Bob Mackie's Designs" exhibition at the Ahmanson Gallery.

Her next television special was *Mitzi...Roarin' in the 20's*, broadcast on March 14, 1976. It was again written by Jerry Mayer with special music material by Dick De Benedictis and Bill Dyer. The show was choreographed and directed by Tony Charmoli; there are Flapper graphics credited to Bill Reinhart.

Gaynor wears two wigs for this period show and performs such numbers as "Running Wild" (music by Arthur Harrington Gibbs, lyrics by Joe Grey and Leo Wood), "I Don't Care" (music by Harry O. Sutton, lyrics by Jean Lenox), "Crazy Words—Crazy Tune" (music by Milton Ager, lyrics by Jack Allen), "Me and My Baby" (music by John Kander, lyrics by Fred Ebb with Ken Berry as The Dream Duo), "I'd Like to Feather My Nest with You" (music by W.R. Williams, lyrics by Lem B. Parker), "The One I Love (Belongs to Somebody Else)" (music by Isham Jones, lyrics by Gus Kahn), "Hard Hearted Hannah, the Vamp of Savannah" (music by Milton Ager, lyrics by Jack Yellen, Bob Bigelow and Charles Bates), "That Crazy Rag" and "Aint Misbehavin'" (music by Thomas "Fats" Waller and Harry Brooks, lyrics by Andy Razaf) and "Everything Old Is New Again" (Peter Allen).

In skits, Gaynor is a married flapper in a montage of her pre-marital wild days, which includes singing the "Vo-do de-o" chorus of "Crazy Words" in a radio show. Gaynor is a fashionable Flapper at a boxing match, a starlet who puts her knees in cement, and a singer at a garden party. In the latter skit, Carl Reiner gets laughs with an annoyed grumble at the starlet's revelation of his illegal dealing and the way he kisses her ring when she offers a hand. In a skit set in a nightclub, Gaynor and Reiner are a married couple who tango as they trade quips. Referring to the violinist, Gaynor asks, "What do you think of his execution?" and Reiner replies, "I'm in favor of it." Gaynor also has a monologue about being a flapper, and another in the Tex's Place sequence.

Linda Hopkins as Miss Bessie of Tex's Place gets two solo numbers, "Ain't Nobody's Business" (by Porter Grainger and Everett Robbins) and "The Birth of the Blues" (by Ray Henderson, with lyrics by Buddy DeSylva and Lew Brown). This gives her a performance running time of four minutes, which was the longest for a Gaynor guest to date. In the "My Baby and Me" number, Charmoli has superimpositions, a mirrored triplicate image, an animated band, animated chorus girl and boy dancers with real girl and boy dancers, an animated plane, ceiling shots with kaleidoscope point of view, and frosted camera. At one point, the animated men appear over Gaynor and the real dancers. Gaynor has a striking entrance framed in a doorway in another outrageous Mackie costume and all this activity does create an appropriate sense of abandon.

For the "Running Wild" medley, Charmoli uses rear projection with black-and-white footage, and for the flapper montage black-and-white cartoon backgrounds with Gaynor among the live actors. "The One I Love (Belongs to Somebody Else)" and "Everything Old Is New Again" have superimpositions and camera flares from Gaynor's costume and earrings.

The show won the Emmy for Outstanding Achievement in Costume Design for Music-Variety and was nominated for Outstanding Directing in a Comedy-Variety or Music Special, Outstanding Writing in a Comedy-Variety or Music Special, Outstanding Achievement in Video Tape Editing for a Special, and Outstanding Achievement in Technical Direction and Electronic Camerawork.

Gaynor reportedly wore 95 costumes. She liked working with Ken Berry, who was great fun; she felt they really "meshed." He had a sense of humor, was a beautiful human being, and a great dancer. Gaynor said that Linda Hopkins was a woman with a voice only God could give. Gaynor had never worked with anyone who sang like that.

Gaynor also praised the innovations that Charmoli brought to this special, saying that he was talented but smart to go to other people to find out what new things could be done on television. Gaynor knew Carl Reiner from *Happy Anniversary* and considered him one of her best friends. One could not do a bad job with Reiner because he was so

8. Mitzi ... The First Time

"together." They did not start shooting their number until late in the day, and by the time they got finally got the perfect take, hours later, their feet were killing them.

Reiner said he was asked by Jack to do the show and commented that Gaynor was put together by somebody who knew how to put people together. According to Reiner, you knew right away there was no airs with her. She was fun, cute, beautiful and sexy.

Charmoli said his vision for the Charleston number was for it to be the best one ever done.

Gaynor toured her act during the 1976 Summer Theatre Straw Hat season; by the time, she had incorporated the Charleston into the show. She was at the Storrowton Theater Eastern States Exposition Park in West Springfield from July 19 to 24, then back at the Westbury Music Fair from July 26 to August 1. From there, Gaynor continued onto Starlight Musicals Concert Program at the H.U. Brown Theatre in Indianapolis. She was then at the South Shore Music Circus in Cohasset, Massachusetts, from September 7 to 12. Later in September, Gaynor was at the Valley Forge Music Fair and then back at Harrah's Headliner Room in Reno. She performed at the Westchester Premiere Theater in Tarrytown, New York, from March 8 to 13, 1977.

Gaynor was interviewed on March 15 by Ike Seamans about audiences. There was no such thing as a bad audience, she claimed. The performer had the responsibility of getting an audience with you. They could be shy, perhaps no one wanting to be the first one to applaud or stand up. You had to know how to temper them and to feel it out. If the show was good, they would like it. It might take a bit longer for them to get with it. But if a show had been on the road a long time and done well in a lot of places, and then it didn't immediately hit with an

Gaynor in *Mitzi ... Roarin' in the 20's* (1976).

audience, you couldn't say the show was now no good. That's not how show business worked.

On the March 25 episode of *The Tonight Show*, Gaynor talked about the struggles with touring seven months in the year, her history of using false eyelashes, days when she was depressed, and meeting Johnny's wife.

Her next TV special was *Mitzi Zings into Spring*, aired on March 27. It was again written by Jerry Mayer with special musical material by Marvin Lourd. The show was choreographed and directed by Tony Charmoli. Gaynor's numbers included "You Make Me Feel Like Dancing" (Leo Sayer and Vini Poncia), "Spring, Spring, Spring" (Johnny Mercer and Gene de Paul), "Isn't It Romantic?" (music by Richard Rodgers, lyrics by Lorenz Hart), "The Springtime Cometh" (E.Y. Harburg and Sammy Fain), "If You Leave Me Now" (Peter Cetera), "Mister Melody" (Chuck Jackson and Marvin Yancy), "Sir Duke" (Stevie Wonder) and "Can We Get Together Again" (Chuck Jackson and Marvin Yancy).

There are two skits. Gaynor and Roy Clark talk about a spring diet where sundaes are used like dueling pistols. The pair sing "We Who are About to Diet" by Bud McCreery. There is also one at an animal singles bar where she, Clark and Wayne Rogers sing Cole Porter's "Let's Do It, Let's Fall in Love." It's a pity we have to endure the bad jokes. The three chorus boys singing and dancing "Let's Do It, Let's Fall in Love" are much more entertaining.

The show opens and closes with location footage of Gaynor in a cornfield planting a garden of gladiola, but otherwise it is studio-bound. Her puffy purple dress may seem unsuitable to wear riding a tractor but she wears a short skirt with T-shirt when planting and watering seeds. The show's non-dancing numbers are "Can We Get Together Again" and "You Are the Sunshine of My Life." In the "You Make Me Feel Like Dancing" medley, gymnasts are initially observed and then incorporated into the number. The gymnast who swings on a pommel horse and a horizontal bar in the background as Gaynor and the chorus boys dance is distracting. Charmoli uses double imagery for the dancing. "Spring, Spring, Spring" has superimposed images, as does the Melting Pot medley, the "Mister Melody" medley, the "Isn't It Romantic?" medley and "Can We Get Together Again." The "Isn't It Romantic?" medley also has a frosted camera. There are camera flares from Gaynor's costumes in "If You Leave Me Now" and "You Are the Sunshine of My Life."

8. Mitzi ... The First Time

The Melting Pot medley comes from Gaynor's stage show. In it, she is funny doing a Dietrich impersonation. Roy Clark gets a solo singing "Danny Boy" (traditional music with lyrics by Frederic Weatherly), complete with reaction shots of Gaynor and Rogers. The climactic "The Yankee Doodle Boy" song and dance also has distracting camera flares from the costumes of the chorus boys. The chorus musical arrangement is addictive and Charmoli's choreography is good. The "Isn't It Romantic?" medley includes Gaynor petting baby animals as her rendition of "Springtime Cometh" is heard on the soundtrack. The dance features another Mackie nude illusion costume of diamonds over a mesh body suit; Charmoli ends on an extreme closeup of Gaynor's eyes. For "If You Leave Me Now" in the medley, she does more of her over-dramatic singing.

Mitzi Zings into Spring won the Emmy for Outstanding Achievement in Costume Design for Music-Variety and was nominated for Outstanding Achievement in Choreography, Outstanding Art Direction for a Comedy-Variety or Music Special and Outstanding Directing in a Comedy-Variety or Music Special. John J. O'Connor of *The New York Times* wrote of Gaynor's determined cuteness, shapely body and shapeless voice.

She reported that all the baby animals in "The Springtime Cometh" pooped on her dress. When Charmoli told her the number was over, Gaynor replied that someone had to take the soiled dress off her. But it was cleaned and subsequently worn again on the road. The gymnasts in the "You Make Me Feel Like Dancing" medley were Olympic athletes.

Gaynor said Roy Clark was terrific, a great talent and a kind and gentle man. Wayne Rogers was an adorable human being. Charmoli reported that when they shot the cornfield sequence, the first take saw the helicopter blow Gaynor over.

Gaynor said that every time they did a TV show, the team wanted it to be an event. Her specials were like hour-long movie musicals. She put everything into them—an awful lot of experience and money. All the specials represented a concept developed over a long period of time. They looked back at their previous specials to see what they had done right and wrong. Gaynor was part of the creative team. There was always something going on in her head about the work.

In April, Gaynor was back at Harrah's in Lake Tahoe, where she performed a Charleston dance.

Mitzi Gaynor

The April edition of *Bon Appetit* magazine featured the article "Mitzi Gaynor—The Star Entertains at Home" by Barbara Wilkins. Gaynor said she maintained her 115-pound figure by working out for an hour at day in the gym in the house, lifting weights. In another interview that year, she elaborated on her secrets to staying young: exercise and much love. She said that her home gym had all the gadgets, slant boards and weights. She did her hour in the morning every morning to get herself going. Jack couldn't stand to see her in the gym so he did his exercises there at night. Gaynor woke up every day feeling great, greeting the Lord, and believing it was so much easier to smile than to frown. It was more manageable living on the West Coast where people were more easygoing, and everyone was into jogging which ironed out a lot of tensions.

In addition to exercise, she put in a rigorous daily dance routine. If Gaynor was performing, it did no harm to work out as well; in fact, she enjoyed it. Gaynor did at least 30 minutes of ballet exercises. Ballet had given her the discipline that was necessary to have a firm body. When she was 21, she was very lazy; at that age, she regarded everything as fun and games. But with time, Gaynor grew up, and discipline grew up with her. You had to be in good shape to look and perform the best.

She didn't eat a big meal before going on stage. You couldn't carry that around for strenuous dance numbers. Gaynor was lucky that she disliked junk food and candy; she didn't eat ice cream or desserts unless she was at the home of a friend. Her only weakness was pasta. Gaynor loved Italian food and she was a great Italian cook.

Time had been very good to her: She had very few wrinkles. She said this was from not wearing foundation cream except for performances. And Gaynor cleansed her face with Neutrogena soap and water. She believed each woman had to acquire her very own look. In her case, Gaynor used a lot of brown eye shadow and loads of lashes. Three times a week, she had a facial.

Another prime factor was sleep. Unless Gaynor had ten hours a night, she felt bad. Whenever Gaynor had to call the doctor, he told her to just get more sleep. He was right, because after a good sleep she was okay again.

Gaynor returned to Westbury from September 13 to 18 and then was back to the Valley Forge Music Fair. In October, she was at Cleveland's Front Row Theatre.

Her next and last TV special was *Mitzi...What's Hot, What's Not,*

8. Mitzi ... The First Time

broadcast on April 6, 1978. It was again written by Jerry Mayer with special music material by Dick De Benedictis and Bill Dyer. The show was choreographed and directed by Tony Charmoli. Gaynor's numbers included "A Hot Time in the Old Town" (music by Theodore August Metz, lyrics by Joe Hayden), "Love Will Find a Way" (De Benedictis and Dyer), "I'm Hip" (Bob Dorough and Dave Frishberg) and "Can't Smile Without You" (Chris Arnold, David Martin and Geoff Morrow).

In one skit, Gaynor and John McCook talk about soap operas and sing "Love Will Find a Way." In another, she and Gavin MacLeod dine at an exclusive restaurant where Gaynor doesn't know how to read the French menu and he's worried about the prices. A third has McCook and MacLeod talking about what they like in a woman and sing Cole Porter's "You're Sensational." *Laugh-In*–style one-liners are intercut into "A Hot Time in the Old Town," including Gaynor's "Does your husband prefer potatoes or store-top stuffing?" as she lies on a stove.

A comic history of the dance includes the gavotte, the waltz, the Charleston and the Hustle. As this segment's narrator, she uses an affected voice. Gaynor's vocal for "I'm Hip" includes scat. Her singing seems to falter in "The Desert Song" (music by Sigmund Romberg, lyrics by Oscar Hammerstein II, Otto Harbach and Frank Mandel), part of a medley.

The non-dancing numbers include "Love Will Find a Way," "Can't Smile Without You" and "You Are the Sunshine of My Life." The jazz medley is leavened by Gaynor's monologues and Benny Goodman's solo "That's a Plenty," where he plays the clarinet with his band. The Goodman number is another rare solo spot in a Gaynor television special, but director Charmoli distracts us with multiple superimpositions.

The Tutmania medley is really a mess. Charmoli opens with a wind-blown parachute, much like the one used for his "Rhapsody in Blue" in *Mitzi...A Tribute to the American Housewife.* There is a Cleopatra snake dance, this time to "(Up a) Lazy River," plus "Swingtown," "The Desert Song," "Dance, Dance, Dance (Yowsah, Yowsah, Yowsah)" and "Tutankhamun." The set is a raised stage which seems to make the performance space unnecessarily small. Charmoli bungles this segment, which is such a shame because, as with his "The Yankee Doodle Boy" in *Mitzi Zings into Spring*, there is so much potential. The disco arrangement is fun, as is the "Tutankhamun" song. Gaynor's various costumes and headdresses give her a new look.

A winking Gaynor with Tutankhamun in *Mitzi ... What's Hot, What's Not* (1978).

8. Mitzi ... The First Time

There is a negative color and flame-edged camera to introduce "A Hot Time in the Old Town" and freeze frames for the number's end. Charmoli uses multiple freeze frames for "Can't Smile Without You" and repeats shots. There are camera flares from the chair in "Love Will Find a Way" as well as flares in the jazz medley, the Tutmania medley and "Can't Smile Without You," which also has superimpositions. He does an optical effect when the legs and then head of Gavin MacLeod appear in a Gaynor monologue. Comic sound effects are heard in the restaurant skit and in for the Tutmania medley.

The show was Emmy-nominated for Outstanding Achievement in Technical Direction and Electronic Camerawork.

The Tutmania segment was said to be inspired by the Treasures of Tutankhamun exhibition then on display at New York's Metropolitan Museum of Art. The "Lazy River" dance was censored because of the Mackie nude illusion costume, with the number restored in 2008 for the TV special *Mitzi Gaynor Razzle Dazzle!: The Special Years*. Gaynor reported that Benny Goodman was unhappy with the set, finding it too artistic, and it was fixed for him. Her repeated use of "You Are the Sunshine of My Life" was how Gaynor felt about the TV audience which had allowed her to go into their homes. She wanted people to say Gaynor was their friend and it came naturally to her because she wasn't playing a part but being herself.

When CBS lost interest in variety shows, Gaynor's star TV career came to an end. Some criticized her choice of guest stars, who were not in the same caliber in their ability to sing and dance. She also rarely gave other performers solo spots. But the shows were created for Gaynor since she was the audience draw.

Gaynor didn't want any drama when making the shows, and she wouldn't work with a choreographer a second time if he believed the show was about him and not her. Tony Charmoli's approach often distracted attention from Gaynor in the specials he directed, but Gaynor had nothing but praise for him.

9

Life After Television

On July 14, 1978, Gaynor was in New York picking the winning ticket in the $2 million Olympic lottery. She returned to the South Shore Music Circus in Cohasset (August 14 to 20 and 22 to 27), the Warwick Musical Theater (August 28 to September 2), the Westbury Music Fair (October 3 to 8) and Cleveland's Front Row Theatre (October 31 to November 5). Her tour also included a run at the Valley Forge Music Fair and in Dallas. A program for the 1978 Gaynor show includes Tutmania in the act. In July 1979, she was at the Tonawanda New York Melody Fair. She performed at the Westbury Music Fair from October 2 to 7 and the Mill Run Theatre in Niles, Illinois, from December 4 to 10.

Gaynor had worked tirelessly throughout the 1970s with television specials and numerous stage appearances. Because she and Jack were so often on the road, her co-workers became a surrogate family. In 1979, Gaynor needed their support more than ever to endure the greatest loss of her life: the death of her mother Pauline. The funeral was held next to a Catholic school and, when Gaynor appeared, all the children and the nuns stood at the windows pointing. Her mother would have been proud. Gaynor bore her grief quietly, and ceremoniously visited Pauline's grave. Pauline would have wanted her daughter to keep performing, so Gaynor returned to work three days after the funeral.

Throughout the 1980s, she celebrated her fifth decade as a performer. Although the golden age of movie musicals was long gone, she was as busy as ever, performing and telling tales about her colorful career on stages across America. Anything that was new, Gaynor would work to her advantage.

Gaynor played the Jones Hall in Houston in March, the Garden

9. Life After Television

State Arts Center in Holmdel, New Jersey, from July 28 to August 2, and the Music Fair in Westbury from October 14 to 19. In April 1981, a badly sprained ankle caused her to cancel a performance in Painter's Hill, Maryland, and a five-day booking in Pittsburgh.

The 1981 Straw Hat Theatre scene saw Gaynor play the Cape Cod Melody Tent in Hyannis from August 3 to 8. She moved to the Atlanta Civic Center where the show program revealed that it was now staged by Thommie Walsh. In 1981, Gaynor was interviewed on Arlene Herson's cable TV show *Getting to Know You*. In the April 1, 1982, *New York Times*, she was interviewed by Albin Krebs and Robert Mcg. Thomas, Jr., for the article "Notes on People; For Mitzi Gaynor, a 28-City Tour Is Restful." She spent eight months on the road, living in motel rooms. This could be a grueling existence for an entertainer, but not for her. Gaynor always got accommodations as luxurious as the towns could provide. She had just begun a week-long run at the Westbury Music Fair in Long Island. Westbury had been a regular stop on her tours since she began them in 1970. It marked the end of a 28-city tour that began last July 7. The touring was necessary to prepare for Gaynor's annual four months at home in Beverly Hills. On tour she kept to a rigid schedule and got plenty of sleep. At home, Gaynor kicked up her heels with Jack, saw all her friends, went to parties and stayed up late. She went on tour to get rest.

She was back at the South Shore Music Circus in Cohasset from June 29 to July 3. On August 10, it was reported that Gaynor had attended Bob Mackie's first complete ready-to-wear collection exhibition, held in the auditorium of New York's Parsons School of Design.

In October, Gaynor played the Front Row Theatre in Cleveland. By 1982, she was netting $250,000 annually from her club engagements. Her address was also listed in the 1981–82 edition of "Map & Guide to the Fabulous Homes of the Stars: Complete Tourist Guide All Points of Interest."

Gaynor was a guest on the Cincinnati TV talk show *The Bob Braun Show* for the episode broadcast on WLWT-TV on August 1, 1984. On March 2, 1985, she attended the Merchants Club for the City of Hope Regal Ball's Second Annual Fashion Achievement Award Salute to Bob Mackie at the Beverly Hilton Hotel.

On July 15, Gaynor was interviewed by Jim Whaley for the Atlanta TV show *Cinema Showcase*. She commented on having been interviewed by Whaley seven times. Gaynor liked to change the format of her shows to

Gaynor in costume for her touring stage show in the 1980s.

give audiences something different and to stop herself from being bored doing the same thing over and over. She had learned from experience what she was able to do but also took ideas from other people about shows. The previous year, Gaynor wanted to do a whole section in the show about Noël Coward. She knew him and he had written about her in some of his books, which was very flattering. Gaynor also loved his music. When she studied classical music as a girl, Gaynor learned some of his songs. Coward's style was arch, pseudo-refined yet classic chic. But after spending a week in rehearsal, she could not do it. No one but Noël Coward could do Noël Coward. So the section was replaced by "Composers I Have Known and Loved." Bob Mackie had moved on to Ready-to-Wear clothes but he was still willing to do her new costumes because Gaynor was the only person still performing this kind of show.

Gaynor appeared in the documentary short *Vancouver: Focus on Expo 86*, written by Chris Aikenhead and directed by Mike Collier. She is seen in the montage of stars performing at the Expo Theatre, singing George Gershwin's "Nashville Nightingale."

The off–Broadway stage musical *Have I Got a Girl for You! (The Frankenstein Musical)*, which opened in New York on October 29, included a reference to her. The show (book by Joel Greenhouse and Penny Rockwell, music and lyrics by Dick Gallagher) was a spoof of the 1935 movie *Bride of Frankenstein*. Baron Von Frankenstein and his evil cohort Dr. Pretorius create the ultimate screen goddess from the assembled body parts of famous Hollywood actresses, which includes Gaynor's lips. The show ran at the Second Avenue Theatre until January 4, 1987.

9. Life After Television

On November 10, Gaynor was honored by the Friars Club as one of the great song-and-dance stars of her generation.

The December 16 *National Enquirer* had an article by Steve Coz entitled "Mitzi Gaynor's Diet & Exercise Secrets." The 55-year-old reported that she was stil using the diet and exercise regimen she used to reduce in 1953. Her best tips: No salt or pepper. They made you retain fluids and made the food so delicious it was hard to turn down. Fruit at least twice a day. Make lunch your big meal of the day so there is ten hours for your body to digest food so it doesn't turn to fat. Have your spouse eat what you eat. If he wants more, let him sneak it out of your sight. Exercise helped to keep the face and chin line firm, strengthened the arms, raised the eyebrows, and helped her maintain a trim waist. Some exercises could be done at home while lying in bed. The best ones were trying to touch your nose with your tongue, rolling the shoulders forward and back, raising your eyebrows once at a time 25 times, and bending to each side 40 times.

From August 3 to 15, 1987, Gaynor performed at the Historic Elitch Theatre in Denver, Colorado.

On September 15, it was reported that a routine exam showed that Gaynor had a brain tumor. She was looking great and performing better than ever on a sellout tour but started experiencing some difficulty hitting the high notes in Denver. Gaynor shrugged it off as a form of altitude sickness in the Mile-High City. But Jack wasn't so sure and asked her when she had her most recent medical checkup. She couldn't remember but promised to see a doctor when back in Los Angeles.

The tumor was found to be benign but if it had gone unchecked, it could have been fatal. It was localized, i.e., it hadn't spread to any vital parts of the brain. And there was a good chance surgery could completely remove it with no chance of a recurrence. She had just completed a two-week record-breaking engagement in Denver when she got the frightening news. Gaynor had to undergo brain surgery. Jack said he would stay by her side until he knew she was all right. He moved into a room in Los Angeles' Cedar Sinai Hospital to be close.

Gaynor didn't want many visitors while she was in hospital; she only wanted people to see her in a positive way. Even though people had been unable to see her, an army of friends stood by. Soon after the surgery, Gaynor's eighth floor hospital suite was filled with flowers, and phone calls poured in. Close friends Zsa Zsa and Eva Gabor, Rossano Brazzi and Milton Berle called. Burt Reynolds called to talk to the girl with the most perfect tush in America. At her request, most of the flowers were sent to the hospital's children's ward.

On October 18, she attended a fashion show at Somper Furs in Beverly Hills where Bob Mackie was honored.

In 1987, Gaynor was on the syndicated TV documentary series *Lifestyles of the Rich and Famous*. The episode featured footage of her singing Irving Berlin's "Blue Skies" at the Terrace Theatre in Long Beach, which demonstrates that the 1987-88 tour was a celebration of Berlin. We see Gaynor and Jack at their Beverly Hills home where they had lived since 1960. Gaynor gardens, cooks, and is seen dressed for a dinner party. Additionally, Bob Mackie talks about her.

The Beans shared their house with a ghost. The ghost was said to be Mrs. Walker, a woman who used to live there and had died there. Gaynor reported that living with a ghost really wasn't very hard. All they had to do was find out her likes and dislikes and go along with them, and then the ghost was very happy. She had never seen Mrs. Walker but Gaynor and Jack had often heard her and felt her presence. And it wasn't only them: A number of the people who had worked for them told how they felt the home was haunted. One houseboy was so frightened that he quit. He said it was just too much to expect him to work and also contend with a ghost.

Mrs. Walker had a very definite taste in chandeliers. If they put up a new one that Mrs. Walker didn't like, she caused it to fall and break; that happened a few times. But if Mrs. Walker liked the chandelier, she took good care of it. She cleaned it regularly and never let it get dusty. At night they could hear the ghost dusting the chandeliers because they tinkled. Gaynor knew it wasn't the wind: They shut every door and window tight and there was no breeze at all, but still the chandelier tinkled. Gaynor said Mrs. Walker never seemed the least bit frightening. She and Jack knew she was there and in fact her presence was actually somewhat comforting.

Karen Kaufman Feder reported on being the star's wardrobe assistant in 1987. Feder went to the interview expecting to meet Gloria Gaynor, the only Gaynor she was familiar with. Disappointed over not working for the disco queen, Feder nonetheless accepted the gig with Mitzi, and within the week was on an airplane en route to the first stop on her national tour—Scranton, Pennsylvania. Karen was responsible for dressing the male chorus line. When the head of wardrobe landed a better gig, Feder also had to serve as

9. Life After Television

Gaynor's personal dresser. Jack scheduled a test run before the evening performance. Bearing Gaynor's opening-number costume, Feder waited outside the dressing room for a few minutes. Then there was a loud, elongated syllable barked from behind the closed door: *"Come!"*

Feder carefully presented the bugle-beaded gown which had an oversized, plastic, center-back zipper. Gaynor stepped into it and directed the girl to zip her up, but she only made it to the star's waistline. It appeared that the gown didn't fit properly. Feder was unaware of the tricky, hidden elastic properties built into it. To her eyes, the only hope of getting the two sides of the zipper to meet would require compressing about four inches of back flesh. Feder began to panic and wondered how she could respectfully word this conundrum. Gaynor's hairdresser was gleefully watching from the dressing room couch. Determined, Feder executed a finger grip on the zipper pull which provided better leverage and the zipper moved up again to reveal a gown that fit perfectly. The gig would prove to be a transitional moment in Feder's life and career.

On March 3, Gaynor attended the Third Annual California Fashion Industry Friends of AIDS Project Los Angeles Benefit Dinner and Fashion Show Honoring Bob Mackie, held at L.A.'s Century Plaza Hotel.

On October 3, she was photographed at a party for the stage show *Anything Goes*. A revival of the show had run on Broadway from October 19, 1987, to September 3, 1989. Gaynor would played the lead role of Reno Sweeney in the national touring production of the Cole Porter musical, directed by Philip Cusack. The choreographer was Tom Mahoney, and Bob Mackie did special costumes for her. It ran for 11 months in 36 cities from 1989 to 1990. The show opened at the Orange County Performing Arts Centre on September 12 and ended in Seattle. Performances included a return to Orange County from January 16 to 21, 1990, and the Bushnell Memorial Hall in Connecticut from May 15 to 20.

Gaynor said the show was very hard for her because she had not been in a play like that on stage in a long time. But it was an interesting experience. She had chosen everyone in the cast so anything that didn't work was her fault. Gaynor loved doing it but said it would take an awful lot to get her to do something akin to it again.

Michael Grossberg in *The Columbus Dispatch* wrote that she was to be admired for her gumption, youth and beauty. But the ingratiating performance consisted of little more than her trademark winks, spins and jiggles, and endless costume changes.

During the 1990s, Gaynor added a new dimension to her career. She became a witty chronicler of Hollywood history in a popular series of columns for the trade paper *The Hollywood Reporter*. Gaynor could recount amazing things from the past and juicy insights. The job came about from her friendship with George Christy, who Gaynor had known as a publicist when he accompanied her to promote *There's No Business Like Show Business*. Gaynor said she mostly wrote about her experiences and the people she worked with. The first article was a retrospective review of Fox's 1936 musical comedy *Pigskin Parade*. Gaynor also wrote about Christy's history, as well as stars Betty Grable, Ginger Rogers, Noël Coward and director George Cukor.

She remained devoted to the care of friends and co-workers. Bob Mackie said that Gaynor was the Angel of Mercy: If you were sick, she would be there with chicken soup and be on the phone with you every day. When Gaynor was losing friends and dancers to HIV, she cooked food and brought it to them.

On June 12, Gaynor was at the opening of *City of Angels* at the Shubert Theater in Century City. A June 16 *New York Times* article by Richard Rosen about Playbill biographies said that her biography for the tour of *Anything Goes* was an example of the tradition of wretched excess. Examples of her criticized statements were a quote from Joshua Logan and one from an advertising executive. "The only thing wrong with Mitzi is that she has so much talent it runs over" and "Mitzi lights up the screen."

In 1991, she appeared on the Starline Hollywood Walk of Fame trading card. Gaynor's Walk of Fame location was 6268 Hollywood Blvd. In 1992, she was the host of the cable television show *American Movie Classics* "Comedy Classics" for 26 weeks.

On October, TNT premiered *Saturday Night Sing-along*, which showed *South Pacific* with the lyrics appearing on the TV screen. An image of her dressed in the sailor suit for "Honey Bun" was used to promote the show.

On February 11, 1996, she was honored at the Professional Dancers Society's 10th Annual Gypsy Awards luncheon held at the Century Plaza Hotel in Century City. In her speech, Gaynor commented that a problem with the '90s was that the women were hard where they should be soft and the men were the opposite.

9. Life After Television

Gaynor and Richard Sabellico in the national tour of *Anything Goes*.

She was referenced in the comedy thriller *Underworld* (1996), written by Larry Bishop and directed by Roger Christian. Ex-con Johnny Crown (Denis Leary) tells his friend Ned Lynch (Larry Bishop) that in prison, he was in *South Pacific* playing the Mitzi Gaynor part.

Johnny added that people said they had never seen the part played with such balls before. Ned asks, "Ballsier even than Mitzi?" Johnny replies. "Oh, yeah." In the film's climax, Ned calls Johnny "Mitzi" and "Nellie Forbush."

It was reported on October 3 that Gaynor had let Arnold Scaasi borrow some of the clothes he had designed for her. They were to be part of his new exhibition of 235 dresses and gowns at the New York Historical Society, "The Joy of Dressing Up: A Retrospective." The clothes included a chain-mail dress of coral and turquoise and a green sequined pants suit. On April 16, 1997, one of the Scaasi dresses she had donated was sold at auction at Sotheby's to benefit the Breast Cancer Research Foundation.

The novel *Breakfast on Pluto* by Patrick McCabe, published by HarperCollins in 1998, centered on Irish Patrick "Pussy" Braden's search for the biological mother who gave him away. The mother is said to look like Gaynor.

Gaynor was interviewed for writer-director Alex Monty Canawati's *All About Alfred* (1998), a documentary about the life and work of film composer Alfred Newman. She was also interviewed for the *Biography* TV episode "The Nicholas Brothers: Flying High," broadcast on the A&E Network on February 23, 1999, and for *Biography*'s "Ethel Merman: There's No Business Like Show Business," broadcast on May 27. On the 100th anniversary of the birth of George Cukor in July, she wrote an article for *The Hollywood Reporter* entitled "Dishing Mr. Cukor," outlining his good and bad attributes. But she outlined the bad things with a wonderful twinkle which made you want to know more.

On March 28, 2001, she dined at Spago's in West Hollywood in a series of final dinners for regulars who represented a "who's who" of old-line Hollywood. The restaurant closed on March 29 after 19 years in business.

Gaynor was the subject of a *Biography* episode broadcast on May 19: "Mitzi Gaynor: Hollywood's Cockeyed Optimist," written by Steven Smith. She was described as a bombshell mix of sex and sass who rose to stardom in the 1950s. Gaynor overcame changing tastes and the passage of time to emerge as a true show business survivor. After half a century of performing, she remained an enduring, energetic symbol of pluck and professionalism. Interviewed for the episode: Gaynor, Jack, Donald O'Connor, Ray Walston, Bob Mackie, Dale Robertson, Robert Sidney, Eddie Bracken, Tony Charmoli and Tom

9. Life After Television

Carlino. The show ended by saying that after seven decades, she continued to embody show business dazzle; a savvy survivor and a caring friend, Gaynor still lived to light up an audience.

In 2001 and 2002 issues of *Films of the Golden Age* magazine, Gaynor was celebrated in a two-part article by Robb Marsh. He had met Mitzi's mother in the late 1960s when they had lunch at Brown Derby in Los Angeles and later went to see Mitzi's star on the Walk of Fame. Marsh also reported seeing Gaynor live at Harrah's Reno Headliner Room in 1968, and attending a taping of *Mitzi Zings into Spring*. In between numbers of the latter, she chatted with him.

On October 11 Gaynor attended "The Thalians Honor Burt Bacharach" at the 48th Annual Ball at Century Plaza Hotel. On November 21, she was at the Academy of Motion Picture Arts and Sciences' Centennial Tribute to Bing Crosby in Beverly Hills. On December 7, Gaynor attended Tony Martin's 90th birthday party at the Friars Club in Beverly Hills.

Gaynor was referenced in Sam Kashner's memoir *When I Was Cool: My Life at the Jack Kerouac School* (HarperCollins, 2004). In the anecdote, Kashner's strait-laced parents took him, Allen Ginsberg and Peter Orlovsky out for a nice kosher dinner at Ratner's, where Ginsberg made Sam's mother swoon by telling her that she reminded him of Gaynor.

On September 17, Gaynor was at the celebrity gala opening for the national tour of *Movin' Out* at the Pantages Theatre in Hollywood. She appeared in the made-for-TV documentary *The Fabulous Fox*, a history of Atlanta's Fox Theatre, released in December 2004.

Gaynor's connection to the novel *Breakfast on Pluto* continued when it was adapted into a 2005 comedy film of the same title, written by Neil Jordan and Patrick McCabe and directed by Jordan. The protagonist is now trans woman Patrick "Kitten" Braden (Cillian Murphy), whose mother Eily Bergin (Eva Birthistle) is said to be the spitting image of Gaynor. Kitten is the love child of Eily and a priest, Father Liam (Liam Neeson), with Eily said to be a blonde housekeeper who looked like the film star with bubble-cut curls. A photograph of Gaynor is seen on the cover of *Picturegoer* magazine, and the beginning of *Les Girls*' "Why Am I So Gone (About that Gal)?" scene is shown on television. Eva Birthistle doesn't look anything like Gaynor, as a subtitled robin says at the film's end. A second robin asks what it knows about Gaynor, to which the first replies, "Nothing. But as Oscar

Wilde said, 'I love to talk about nothing. It's the only thing I know anything about.'" Jordan reported that he asked to use a *South Pacific* clip but the Rodgers and Hammerstein estate refused permission, so he used *Les Girls* instead.

On August 26, Gaynor attended a vegetarian lunch honoring Dick Van Dyke at the Universal Hilton Hotel. "A Celebration of Caring" highlighted the actor's regular appearances for the Midnight Mission in Los Angeles; he had raised over $5 million for them. The event was hosted by Actors and Others for Animals.

On October 14, the New York Alumni adopted Gaynor as an official New Yorker at Beverly Hills High School. New York City mayor Michael Bloomberg issued a proclamation paying tribute to her distinguished career as a singer, dancer, actress and writer. On November 7, she guested on ABC-TV's *Good Morning America*, shot in New York. On November 8, Gaynor, Shirley Jones and Rita Moreno were interviewed for Movieguy.com about the Rodgers & Hammerstein Collection DVD. When the talk came to drag queens, she said no one had done her in drag but Gaynor was always in drag anyway.

Gaynor found happiness in her home life with Jack Bean for over four decades. Their personal and professional relationship was unique in Hollywood for its longevity and success. On December 4, he died of pneumonia in the couple's Beverly Hills home, at age 84. *Variety* reported in its obituary that for the past several years, Jack had been producing Mitzi's lecture series and personal appearance tours and was in the midst of developing a new act to tour the country. In addition to Mitzi, Jack was survived by a daughter.

Gaynor didn't know if she could be Mitzi Gaynor any more without Jack because they were like one person. But she soon became involved in various charitable initiatives, including the Professional Dancers Society, where she served as president. The organization helped both active and inactive professional dancers. With the Actors Fund of America, they provided low-income housing, retirement and nursing facilities for entertainment professionals. Gaynor said the society helped dancers in need, especially older dancers who couldn't quite make it any more and had no support. There was no Motion Picture Relief Fund Home for dancers, and the Society didn't take young people because they still had a chance to work.

Bob Mackie said that Mitzi's dancers loved her because she was fun and supportive and brought a lot of love into the room. Tony

9. Life After Television

Charmoli added that Gaynor came to work as one of them, not as a star, and giggled and made mistakes with them. The Society held an annual show, guided by Gaynor, for and about dancers.

In 2006, she was interviewed for a chapter in Rose Eichenbaum's book *The Dancer Within: Intimate Conversations with Great Dancers* (Wesleyan University Press, 2008). Gaynor said she stayed in good shape because of all the choreographers she had worked with. She still had a good back and only occasionally had aches and pains. She wanted to take her show on the road again with just an orchestra and herself. Gaynor wanted to tell stories from her life, sing, do sketches, and change her clothes on the stage behind a screen. She didn't want to retire because she had such a good time doing shows.

On April 10, 2007, Gaynor was honored by the Museum of Television & Radio in Los Angeles with a special evening celebrating her TV specials. There was a screening of the documentary *Mitzi Gaynor Razzle-Dazzle!: The Special Years*, directed by David Stern. It features interviews with Gaynor, Bob Mackie, Carl Reiner, Tony Charmoli and dancers Alton Ruff and Randy Doney. After the screening, there was a panel discussion with her, Mackie and Charmoli. In conjunction with the event, the museum also featured a month-long gallery exhibit, "Mitzi by Mackie." It featured Mackie's costumes from her specials along with a selection of costumes from Gaynor's stage shows and concert appearances.

She was interviewed for the documentary short *Mitzi Gaynor: Impressions of the Fox Years*, released on November 17, 2007, on the DVD of *Damon Runyon's Bloodhounds of Broadway*. The short was written and directed by Lisa Van Eyssen. On July 25, she was interviewed by Bruce Vilanch for "A Salute to Miss Mitzi Gaynor" at San Francisco's Castro Theatre. On July 30, she appeared on "The Academy of Television Arts and Sciences TV Moves Live," a celebration of 60 years of dance on television. She sang the final few bars of "Poor Papa." On November 13, she attended the West Coast premiere of *Mitzi Gaynor: Razzle Dazzle! The Special Years* at the Leonard H. Goldenson Theatre in North Hollywood.

On November 18, *Mitzi Gaynor Razzle Dazzle!: The Special Years* was broadcast on PBS. It had the tagline "Before there was *Dancing with the Stars*, there was Mitzi Gaynor!" It won the Emmy for Outstanding Entertainment Programming/Special. Gaynor said it was ironic as she had not been Emmy-nominated for any of the specials when they were broadcast.

10

Razzle Dazzle! My Life Behind the Sequins

On January 10, 2009, Gaynor's one-woman show *Razzle Dazzle! My Life Behind the Sequins,* an intimate evening of love, laughs and music, debuted at San Francisco's Herbst Theatre. The idea for the show came after she decided it was time to get rid of some of the hundreds of costumes she kept in storage. She called around for help with the sale, which led to a special evening honoring her career, a display of her Mackie costumes and a documentary about her life. The show was said to include her often hilarious recollections of famous friends and co-stars, and behind-the-scenes anecdotes from Gaynor's life and career. These were accompanied by archive footage and personal photos. She also sang songs including "There's No Business Like Show Business," "Honey Bun," "I'm Gonna Wash That Man Right Outa My Hair," "Some Enchanted Evening," "A Wonderful Guy" and "You Are the Sunshine of My Life." Gaynor had seven costume changes. At one point she joked about the public perception of her: "Mitzi Gaynor? My God, is she still alive?" Gaynor said the show had a rough outline, because the band had to know which songs to play, but the stories might change night to night, depending on the audience. It toured around the United States.

On March 7, Gaynor was honored at Swellegance, the Boston Youth Moves Ninth Annual fundraiser at the Westin Copley Place. She was the recipient of the Lifetime Achievement Award presented by Honorary Event Chair Chita Rivera.

Gaynor participated in the documentary *Passion, Prejudice and* South Pacific*: Creating an American Masterpiece.* This was featured on the Blu-ray of the 50th Anniversary edition of *South Pacific,* released on March 31. On May 5, she attended a celebration of the

Blu-ray release held at the Lincoln Center Barnes & Noble in New York City.

On June 7, Gaynor attended The Actors Fund event honoring Chita Rivera at their 13th Annual Tony Awards Party. Rivera received the Julie Harris Award for Lifetime Achievement. The event was held at Hollywood' Skirball Center. On June or July 21 she attended "The Academy of Television Arts & Sciences TV Moves Live 2" at the Wadsworth Theater in Los Angeles. The show featured a dance tribute to Michael Jackson. On July 10, Gaynor was honored with the Tremaine 2009 Entertainer of the Year award. This came from the Joe Tremaine dance competition nationals final gala, held at the Renaissance Orlando Hotel at Sea World, Florida.

On November 1, Gaynor was at the 54th Annual Thalians Ball at the Beverly Hilton Hotel; it honored Mickey Rooney and the USO Shows for America's Armed Forces around the world. The show was taped for TV and directed by David McKenzie.

On November 7, she received Chapman University's Lifetime Achievement in the Arts award during the 28th annual American celebration gala night at Chapman University in Orange, California. In response to the gala evening's stage show, Gaynor exclaimed, "This show should be at the Pantages Theater right now!"

On April 13, 2010, she was honored with the Bob Harrington Lifetime Achievement Award at the 25th Annual Bistro Awards, held at the Gotham Comedy Club in New York. On April 18, when *Mitzi Gaynor: Razzle Dazzle! The Special Years* won its Emmy, she was performing at the Keith C. and Elaine Johnson World Performing Arts Center at Lynn University in Boca Raton.

Her one-woman show came to New York on May 18; it was her first New York nightclub appearance in years. It ran at Feinstein's at Loews Regency until May 29. Stephen Holden in *The New York Times* noted that Gaynor's singing voice was now little more than a wobbly squeak that sounded especially vulnerable when applied to a four-song medley from *South Pacific*. She continued to tour the show into 2014, including a stop in Vancouver.

On May 23, Gaynor was a presenter at the 55th Annual Drama Desk Awards, held at the F.H. LaGuardia Concert Hall at Lincoln Center in New York. On June 2, she attended the opening night performance of *South Pacific* at the Center Theatre Group's Ahmanson Theatre in Los Angeles. On June 5 Gaynor was at SHARE's 57th Annual BOOMTOWN Event, held at the Santa Monica Civic

Auditorium. It was a benefit for at-risk youth. On June 25, she attended a screening of a recently restored 70mm print of *South Pacific* at the Samuel Goldwyn Theater in Beverly Hills. The event was held by the Academy of Motion Picture Arts and Sciences in association with Center Theater Group. Following the screening, she and the Center's artistic director Michael Ritchie discussed the film onstage.

A January 16, 2011, interview with Rita Moreno referenced her. The 79-year-old Moreno remained busy with her one-woman show between acting jobs and said that she and other icons like Gaynor were great for still doing one-woman shows. That was the difference between them and people who didn't do *anything* at their age.

On September 10, Gaynor was a presenter at *2011 Primetime Creative Arts Emmy Awards,* held at the Nokia Theatre Los Angeles and telecast on September 17. The show was written by Guy Nicolucci and directed by Chris Donovan. On December 12, it was reported that she would participate in a three-show concert series at the Reagle Music Theatre of Greater Boston. *Razzle Dazzle!: My Life Behind the Sequins* would begin on April 15 at the Robinson Theatre in Waltham.

On December 18, Gaynor was given the 2011 Mary Pickford Award for Outstanding Contribution to the Entertainment Industry at *The 16th Annual Satellite Awards,* held at the Beverly Hills Hotel. The show was written by Quendrith Johnson and directed by Ivan Andrijanic and Mirjana Van Blaricom and broadcast as a television special. Interviewed on the red carpet, Gaynor reported she met Pickford as a little girl. She also said she was writing a book about herself; it was hard to write, but she was having fun remembering her life.

Gaynor donned her *South Pacific* "Honey Bun" costume to attend a screening of the film.

10. Razzle Dazzle! My Life Behind the Sequins

Gaynor was interviewed for writer-director Jo Ann Young's PBS film *Oscar Hammerstein II—Out of My Dreams*, telecast on March 3. Later in the month, she hosted the Professional Dancers Society 25th Anniversary Gypsy Awards Gala Luncheon honoring Julie Andrews, held at the Beverly Hilton Hotel. In footage from the event, Gaynor is funny recalling the five years of negotiating with Andrews' manager to get her to attend. Gaynor admits to going for a Kim Kardashian look in her outfit but came out more like Sophie Tucker. When she comically lies about her age, someone in the audience makes a comment which leads her to reply, "I heard that, you bitch." Andrews says that Gaynor needs to take her comedy routine on the road, and that her (Andrews') manager would love to talk to her about it.

She participated in the television special *Reel Life: Marilyn Monroe*, broadcast on August 4. Gaynor was interviewed for the Academy of Television Arts and Sciences' biographical history series *The Interviews: An Oral History of Television*, broadcast on October 12. The two-hour-plus interview was conducted by John Dalton on October 9 in Beverly Hills. This interview is particularly good in discussing Gaynor's TV guest appearances. She reported that she was currently writing her book, entitled *Have I Told You This Lately?* Gaynor began doing her one-woman show again in February in Delaware, and continued across the country. She was accompanied by her agents on the road. Gaynor had become wealthy from touring. She liked to tour, only having to work two hours a night, and otherwise got to visit friends. One tour had her appear on a ship, which was fun. Gaynor found audiences to be ever better now than they had been in the old days. One lady said she loved Gaynor because she (the lady) grew up with her.

Gaynor observed how television had changed, with the use of profanity now more acceptable. There was not as much of her kind of music performed in show business, the kind of music she grew up on, apart from people like Tony Bennett. Performers were more permissive than Gaynor liked. She was not a puritan but had been brought up to believe that you didn't do certain things. A lot of new performers went out there with no experience and costs were higher. But nobody seemed to have any real guts and sometimes new performers lacked good advisors. They had no one to tell them not to do certain things if you wanted to last in the business. You had to have respect. Gaynor gave Robert Downey, Jr., as an example. He had a drug problem and the media gave him a hard time. But the actor survived and was now even better. Gaynor was very proud of him.

Gaynor saw herself as an artiste. She was proud to say that as a celebrity, she always went out in public clean and looking good. She had self-respect but that could be due to being a Virgo as well. Gaynor also didn't want to hurt anybody. Her proudest professional achievement was doing this interview and she loved that it was being done. Gaynor said she would like to be remembered as a friend.

In December, Gaynor was interviewed by Michael Portantiere for *Life After 50* magazine. In the article, "The Cockeyed Optimism of Mitzi Gaynor," the 81-year-old said she didn't think she had ever admitted to being over 50. Gaynor was still writing a book about her life but finding it difficult. She found Christmas without Jack hard. They used to throw an annual party the Sunday before with food that she prepared herself.

She attributed her vigor, great shape and legs to having been a dancer since childhood and also keeping fit with a regular exercise regimen. She had a gym in one of her garages, with a stationary bike, treadmill and weights. Three or four times a week, Gaynor did Callanetics, a system of exercise developed by Callan Pinckney, who had produced an exercise tape for people with bad backs.

Gaynor didn't spend much time at home because she was always working (and also honored an awful lot, which she found to be weird and wondrous). She was also kept busy as the president of the Professional Dancers Society. She no longer went to the movies but had them sent to her to watch at home. On TV, she liked *Modern Family* and *Dancing with the Stars*. Cooking remained a favorite pastime, and the article included her holiday recipes. The appetizer was Duck Pâté *à la* Mitzi Bean, the main course Pork Loin with Green Peppercorn Sauce, and the dessert Chocolate-Pumpkin Layer Cake with Brown-Sugar Frosting. Jack had taught her that life was as good as you made it, and she remained a cockeyed optimist.

Gaynor was interviewed by Betsy Price for the *USA Today* article "Stage legend Mitzi Gaynor dishes on her Hollywood life" (February 19). She was then performing her one-woman show at the DuPont Theatre in Wilmington, Delaware. Gaynor had taken a break from touring in 2010 to cruise around the world. But while she was planning it, every time she turned on the TV, some movie version of the *Titanic* was playing. The tour resumed in 2011, and among the stops that year

10. Razzle Dazzle! My Life Behind the Sequins

were Florida, Ohio, South Carolina, California and Nevada. She still felt the loss of Jack, and continued to wear her wedding ring with his, attached to a bracelet tucked under her jacket sleeve.

On March 19, Gaynor attended a screening of *South Pacific* at Chicago's Music Box Theatre. The evening also included a pre-screening talk with film historian and author Leonard Maltin. When an audience member shouted, "Sing for us!" Gaynor replied that he had to come and see her show. She added, "I'm a Hungarian. I don't sing for nothing." Standing to tell one story, Gaynor was a bit wobbly, which hinted at the trouble she would later have with her legs. She told a funny story about doing a telethon where an elderly lady said that *her* mommy and daddy loved Gaynor.

On April 1, at the Hollywood Legends Auction Preview, her dresses were on display at Julien's Auctions Gallery in Beverly Hills. On May 15, she was the main attraction at Michael Feinstein's new San Francisco club, Feinstein's at the Nikko.

On June 9, Gaynor attended the Actors Fund's 17th annual Tony Awards viewing party in Hollywood. The event was broadcast as an episode of the TV news talk show *Red Carpet Report* on June 10.

On September 17, it was announced that the 82-year-old was selling her Beverly Hills home. The two-story Spanish-style casa, built in 1929, had five bedrooms, six bathrooms and a pool. It was 4167 square feet and the asking price was $5.5 million.

The home's original details included the groin-vaulted entry loggia, Spanish tile and Parquet de Versailles–style wood flooring, beamed ceiling in the living room, leaded glass skylights, casement windows and French doors. The center hall entry had a wrought iron railed staircase. There was a generously proportioned formal living room with a black marble fireplace, and a large dining room for entertaining. The sunroom with a row of oversized arched windows led out to a red-brick dining terrace that was shaded by an awning and overlooked the backyard and swimming pool.

The kitchen had bull-nosed granite counter tops and raised panel cabinetry. It featured a small center work island, a high-end commercial-style six-burner range, and an adjacent butler's pantry lined with glass-fronted upper cabinets. Like many older homes in the Flats of Beverly Hills, there was a staff bedroom and bathroom tucked back into the service area behind the kitchen. The nearby breakfast room was an exquisite—if Old School—jewel box with honey-toned

Gaynor still performing in the 2010s.

Venetian plaster walls, original casement windows, a built-in buffet with leaded glass details, and an antique crystal chandelier.

There were two guest-family bedrooms upstairs plus a super-sized master suite. The latter encompassed a bedroom chamber and adjoining sitting room, a Juliet balcony that overlooked the backyard, and a closet-lined dressing room with a roomy walk-in closet. A fourth potential bedroom-library with private bathroom was located on the main floor. The same graphic striped fabric was applied to the walls, the roll-armed divan, the patio-like chair cushions and the curtains. It was also stuck to at least three of the four walls in the attached bathroom. As this sort of decor just wasn't done any more, it was a marvelous little decorative time capsule.

Gaynor was in the British television documentary *Hello: A Portrait of Leslie Phillips*, broadcast on September 28. It was written and directed by Jules Williams and Rosemary Reed. Gaynor talked about the making of *Les Girls*, in which Phillips appeared.

On October 27, she discussed her film career at the Edgerton Center for the Performing Arts in Fairfield, Connecticut. It was reported on January 7, 2014, that Gaynor's Beverly Hills home sold for $4.9 million. On January 25, she attended the Nevada Ballet Theatre Woman of the Year Black and White Ball at Aria in Las Vegas. On March 30, she presided over the Professional Dancers Society's 27th Annual Gypsy Award luncheon at the Beverly Hilton Hotel. That year it honored Leslie Caron and choreographer Dee Dee Wood.

TCM A Salute to Mitzi Gaynor was broadcast on May 12. Interviewed by Robert Osborne, she spoke about *The Joker Is Wild*, *Les Girls*, *The I Don't Care Girl*, *Mitzi ... A Tribute to the American Housewife* and *Golden Girl*. Gaynor nicknamed Osborne "Bobby O."

Gaynor was interviewed for the biographical documentary *Mia, a Dancer's Journey*, broadcast on PBS on November 20. The film was written by Maria Ramas and directed by Ramas and Kate Johnson. On December 9, she attended a screening of *There's No Business Like Show Business* for its 60th anniversary at the Regent Theatre in Los Angeles.

A Gaynor quote appeared on the back cover of the book *Make 'Em Laugh: Short-Term Memories of Longtime Friends* by Debbie Reynolds and Dorian Hannaway. Gaynor wrote that the book was just like Debbie: affectionate, unforgettable, and laugh-out-loud funny.

On September 10, Gaynor was honored with the inaugural Legend Award from Nigel Lythgoe's Dizzy Feet Foundation at the Sixth

Annual Celebration of Dance Gala in Los Angeles. By this time, she was using a wheeled walker although she could stand up to be photographed.

In 2016, the Official Mitzi Gaynor Home Page was created with a biography, news about appearances, photos and listings of movie and TV appearances. The site also had links to YouTube, Facebook, Instagram and Twitter.

Gaynor reported that the first half of 2017 was a little challenging. She dealt with a circulatory issue in her legs that required several surgeries. In February, she announced that the circulation had now been fully restored in both legs. Gaynor was in physical therapy to get back to work and back in her heels. She had a new show in the works and new songs to sing.

On March 26, *The Hollywood Reporter* published an article by her (as told to Scott Feinberg) on the March 6 passing of Robert Osborne. On September 9, it was reported that she had provided the foreword for the book *Starring the Plaza* by Patty Farmer, published by Beaufort Books. Gaynor also disclosed a few of her own adventures at the iconic hotel.

On September 30, she was inducted into the Great American Songbook Hall of Fame by its founder Michael Feinstein. The Hall of Fame celebrated lyricists, composers and performers who helped to create "the soundtrack of our lives" with their contributions to American popular song. Gaynor announced the donation of her own extensive collection of musical charts and other memorabilia to the Foundation's archives. She was also interviewed by Feinstein. Gaynor reported that Irving Berlin wanted her to do a road company of *Annie Get Your Gun* but she declined, wanting to do her own show.

In late April 2018, shortly after moving into an apartment, she had minor surgery on one of her feet. On June 26, Gaynor attended the 60th anniversary screening of *South Pacific*, hosted by the TCL Chinese Theatre in Hollywood. She also was in conversation with Susan King. Gaynor talked about her vascular problems (she almost lost both legs), and how her left leg was still an issue. The head of the Beverly Hills Rehabilitation Center saved her life by insisting the legs be not cut off.

On February 1, 2019, Gaynor was interviewed by Leonard Maltin and Jessie Maltin for their podcast *Maltin on Movies*. She had allowed Leonard to read three chapters of her memoir, and he thought they were very good. He learned things, was amused by some of the anecdotes and thought people would get a kick out of it.

Gaynor was in the comedy documentary *Funny You Never Knew*, which focused on three comics from the 1950s: Imogene Coca, George Gobel and Martha Raye. It had multiple writers and was directed by Andrew Hunt. It was released theatrically on March 28.

On August 3, she was the special guest for "Michael Feinstein Sings Cole Porter" at the Los Angeles County Arboretum & Botanic Garden. Feinstein was accompanied by the Pasadena Symphony Pops. There is footage of Feinstein and Gaynor singing "You're the Top."

Gaynor was interviewed by Katie Bruno for the article "Mitzi Gaynor—Still a Dynamo at 88" in the September 30 issue of *Closer Weekly*. She revealed that her future plans included a Turner Classics Movie cruise in October, her one-woman show, an auction and the publication of her memoir in 2020.

On October 6, Gaynor was on *CBS News Sunday Morning*. By this point, she appeared to be a less vibrant woman; she didn't move around the way she used to because of a badly hurt leg. It had been quite some time since she had been able to dance but she wanted to dance again. She also wanted to look good and feel good because she felt that a lot of people were waiting for her to come back. Gaynor also spoke about being wooed by Howard Hughes, landing the starring role in *South Pacific* and sharing the *Ed Sullivan Show* stage with The Beatles. In addition, viewers saw her career scrapbooks. She commented that host Mo Rocca and producer Jay Kernis were kind and thoughtful.

From October 23 to 26, Gaynor was on the Turner Classic Movies Classic Cruise. For the Halloween costume party "come as your favorite movie character," she went as Nellie Forbush dressed for "Honey Bun."

On November 16, Gaynor was part of the PBS special *A Classic Christmas*. On December 4, she received a Medal of Honor from the Actors Fund for her work in the Professional Dancers Society. There was a public preview on December 6 of the auction of her costumes and memorabilia in the Los Angeles Bonham gallery. She attended a Q&A on December 8 before the auction on December 10. The event was done in partnership with Turner Classic Movies.

On February 12, 2020, *Variety* published an article by Gaynor on Kirk Douglas, who had died on February 5. In the article, "Kirk Douglas' Former Co-Star, Mitzi Gaynor, on How He Was Always 'the Ragman's Son,'" she described working with him on *For Love or Money*.

In June, Bonhams had an online sale of costumes, couture and memorabilia from her archive collection with the proceeds to benefit yhe Actors Fund.

Gaynor was in director Mariem Pérez Riera's *Rita Moreno: Just a Girl Who Decided to Go for It*. The biographical documentary premiered at the Sundance Film Festival on January 29, 2021. In Gaynor's interview, which took place on February 1, 2019, she talked about how the studios had contract actresses like Gaynor and Moreno go with men on "pretend" dates for publicity. Gaynor was seen in photos with Donald O'Connor and Richard Brown Coyle.

In March 2022, Gaynor was the subject of "In the Archives with Michael Feinstein: Women's History Month." The episode included an interview from her 2017 Songbook Hall of Fame induction and a look at some of her materials, housed in the Songbook Library & Archives.

In June, she moved into a new home. Gaynor decided, rather than keep things in storage, to have an auction. The Private Collection was auctioned by Andrew Jones Auctions on June 29. She also reported that her autobiography was still being written despite delays.

Gaynor was in the French documentary *Dream Girl: The Making of Marilyn Monroe*, written and directed by Ian Ayres. It premiered on August 6 at the TLC Chinese Theatre in Hollywood.

On September 1, she was honored with the Legacy Award by the 58th Annual Cinecon Classic Film Festival at the Hollywood Legion Theatre. She was glad to still have her life, her friends, and some talent left. The event led an interview by Michael Feinstein with her and a Q&A before a screening of *Anything Goes*.

Gaynor is in the documentary *Bob Mackie: Naked Illusion* (2024), written and directed by Mathew Miele and released on May 13, 2024. She was interviewed for the film in October 2019.

On August 29, Book Guild Publishing released *A Happy Man: In Conversation with Rossano Brazzi*. Regrettably any content relating to *South Pacific* could not be accessed in time to be included in this book. Gaynor's agents advised in September that she still was at work on her memoir, though it would not be out this year.

11

Death

Gaynor died from natural causes in her Los Angeles home on October 17, 2024, at age 93. This was first reported by her agents on her Instagram, Facebook and X pages. They wrote that she was a vibrant and extraordinary woman; a caring and loyal friend; and a warm, gracious, very funny and altogether glorious human being. And she could cook, too! The agents also noted that Gaynor truly enjoyed every moment of her professional career and the great privilege of being an entertainer.

The New York Times obituary by Anita Gates was headlined "Leading Lady of Movie Musicals." Wrote Gates, "The bubbly actress, singer and dancer … landed one of the most coveted movie roles of the mid-20th century, the female lead in 'South Pacific,' but … abandoned film as the era of movie musicals came to an end."

Mike Barnes and Duane Byrge of the *Hollywood Reporter* wrote that she was a "leggy entertainer" with "saucy vitality" and "exuberant singing and dancing." They noted her success as a Las Vegas headliner and centerpiece of annual TV specials and stated that donations in her memory could be made to the Entertainment Community Fund and the Great American Songbook Foundation.

Gaynor had no immediate family members who survived her.

Appendix of Work

Works are listed in chronological order.

Stage

Song Without Words: The Life and Times of Peter Ilyich Tchaikovsky (date unknown). San Francisco.
Roberta (1946). Civic Light Opera Association, Los Angeles.
The Gypsy Lady (1946). Civic Light Opera Association. Los Angeles, New York.
Song of Norway (1947). Civic Light Opera Association. Los Angeles, Philadelphia.
Louisiana Purchase (1947). Civic Light Opera Association. Los Angeles.
Naughty Marietta (1948). Civic Light Opera Association. Los Angeles.
The Great Waltz (1949). Civic Light Opera Association. Los Angeles.
Jollyanna (August 8 to September 1952). Civic Light Opera Association–Curran Theater, San Francisco; (September to October 1952) Philharmonic Theater, Los Angeles, as Penny
Anything Goes (national tour, 1989–90) as Reno Sweeney.
Razzle Dazzle! My Life Behind the Sequins (national tour, 2009–10, 2011–14) as Herself.

Shorts

It's Your Health (1949) as Peggy Hendricks (billed as Mitzi Gerber).
South Pacific *on the Screen, A Perfect Hit*. Movietone News (1958) as Herself.
The Children of Lindos (1960) as Herself.
Vancouver: Focus on Expo 86 (1986). Part: Herself.
Mitzi Gaynor: Impressions of the Fox Years (2007) as Herself.

Films

My Blue Heaven (1950) as Gloria Adams.
Take Care of My Little Girl (1951) as Adelaide Swanson.

Appendix of Work

Golden Girl (1951) as Lola Crabtree.
We're Not Married! (1952) as Patricia "Patsy" Reynolds Fisher.
Damon Runyon's Bloodhounds of Broadway (1952) as Emily Ann Stackerlee.
The I Don't Care Girl (1953) as Eva Tanguay.
Down Among the Sheltering Palms (1953) as Rozouila.
Three Young Texans (1954) as Rusty Blair.
There's No Business Like Show Business (1954) as Katie aka Katy Donahue.
Jamboree (1954) as Herself.
Anything Goes (1956) as Patsy Blair.
The Birds and the Bees (1956) as Jean Harris.
The Joker Is Wild (1957) as Martha Stewart.
Les Girls (1957) as Joanne "Joy" Henderson.
South Pacific (1958) as Ensign Nellie Forbush.
Happy Anniversary (1959) as Alice Walters.
Surprise Package (1960) as Gabby Rogers.
For Love or Money (1963) as Kate Brasher.
All About Alfred (1998) as Herself.
The Fabulous Fox (2004) as Herself.
Passion, Prejudice and South Pacific*: Creating an American Masterpiece* (March 31, 2009) as Herself.
Funny You Never Knew (2019) as Herself.
Rita Moreno: Just a Girl Who Decided to Go for It (2021) as Herself.
Dream Girl: The Making of Marilyn Monroe (2022) as Herself.

Television

The George Jessel Show (September 13, 1953) as Herself.
The 26th Annual Academy Awards (March 25, 1954) as Herself.
A Star Is Born World Premiere (September 29, 1954) as Herself.
Here Comes Donald (October 9, 1954) as Herself.
Toast of the Town (December 5, 1954) as Herself.
Here Comes Donald (January 8, 1955) as Herself.
The Ed Sullivan Show (April 8, 1956) as Herself.
The 30th Annual Academy Awards (March 26, 1958) as Herself.
Reflets de Cannes (May 3, 1958). Part: Herself.
Reflets de Cannes (May 11, 1958) as Herself.
The Ed Sullivan Show (June 15, 1958) as Herself.
The George Jessel Show (January 13, 1959) as Herself.
The Jack Benny Hour (March 18, 1959) as Herself.
The 31st Annual Academy Awards (April 6, 1959) as Herself.
The Frank Sinatra Timex Show (October 19, 1959) as Herself.
The Dick Clark Show (January 30, 1960) as Herself.
The 32nd Annual Academy Awards (April 4, 1960) as Herself.
Here Comes Donald (October 11, 1960) as Herself.

Appendix of Work

The 33rd Annual Academy Awards (April 17, 1961) as Herself.
The Ed Sullivan Show (February 16, 1964) as Herself.
Danny Thomas Special: My Home Town (February 6, 1966) as Herself.
The Tonight Show Starring Johnny Carson (February 10, 1967) as Herself.
The Tonight Show Starring Johnny Carson (February 15, 1967) as Herself.
The 39th Annual Academy Awards (April 10, 1967) as Herself.
The Tonight Show Starring Johnny Carson (December 7, 1967) as Herself.
Lighting of the Rockefeller Christmas Tree (December 7, 1967) as Herself.
The Kraft Music Hall: "Mitzi Gaynor Christmas Show" (December 20, 1967) as Herself.
The Bob Hope Special (October 14, 1968) as Herself.
Rowan & Martin's Laugh-In (October 14, 1968) as Herself.
Mitzi (October 14, 1968) as Herself.
The Tonight Show Starring Johnny Carson (September 17, 1969) as Herself.
The Bob Hope Special (October 13, 1969) as Herself.
Rowan & Martin's Laugh-In (October 13, 1969) as Herself.
Mitzi's 2nd Special (October 13, 1969) as Herself.
The Tonight Show Starring Johnny Carson (July 16, 1970) as Herself.
The Merv Griffin Show (December 10, 1970) as Herself.
Perry Como's Winter Show (December 9, 1971) as Herself.
The 24th Annual Primetime Emmy Awards (May 14, 1972) as Herself.
The Tonight Show Starring Johnny Carson (May 19, 1972) as Herself.
The Tonight Show Starring Johnny Carson (September 29, 1972) as Herself.
The Tonight Show Starring Johnny Carson (March 23, 1973) as Herself.
Cavalcade of Champions (March 27, 1973) as Herself.
Mitzi ... The First Time (March 28, 1973) as Herself.
Mitzi ... A Tribute to the American Housewife (February 4, 1974) as Herself.
The 1974 Annual Las Vegas Entertainment Awards (November 20, 1974) as Herself.
Bicentennial Minutes (March 17, 1975) as Narrator.
The Tonight Show Starring Johnny Carson (March 21, 1975) as Herself.
Mitzi and 100 Guys (March 24, 1975) as Herself.
Mitzi ... Roarin' in the 20's (March 14, 1976) as Herself.
The Tonight Show Starring Johnny Carson (March 25, 1977) as Herself.
Mitzi Zings into Spring (March 27, 1977) as Herself.
Mitzi ... What's Hot, What's Not (April 6, 1978) as Herself.
The American Guild of Variety Artists 10th Annual Entertainer of the Year Awards (January 23, 1980) as Herself.
Getting to Know You (1981) as Herself.
Cinema Showcase (July 15, 1985) as Herself.
Lifestyles of the Rich and Famous (1987) as Herself.
American Movie Classics: "Comedy Classics" (1992) as Herself.
Biography. "The Nicholas Brothers: Flying High" (February 23, 1999) as Herself.

Appendix of Work

Biography. "Ethel Merman: There's No Business Like Show Business" (May 27, 1999) as Herself.
Biography. "Mitzi Gaynor: Hollywood's Cockeyed Optimist" (May 19, 2001) as Herself.
Mitzi Gaynor Razzle Dazzle!: The Special Years (November 18, 2008) as Herself.
The 54th Annual Thalians Ball (October 20, 2009) as Herself.
2011 Primetime Creative Arts Emmy Awards (September 17, 2011) as Herself.
The 16th Annual Satellite Awards (December 18, 2011) as Herself.
Oscar Hammerstein II—Out of My Dreams (March 3, 2012) as Herself.
Reel Life: Marilyn Monroe (August 4, 2012) as Herself.
The Interviews: An Oral History of Television (October 12, 2012) as Herself.
Red Carpet Report: "The Actors Fund Tony Viewing Party" (June 10, 2013) as Herself.
Hello: A Portrait of Leslie Phillips (September 28, 2013) as Herself.
TCM Salute to Mitzi Gaynor (May 12, 2014) as Herself.
Mia, a Dancer's Journey (November 20, 2014) as Herself.
CBS News Sunday Morning (October 6, 2019) as Herself.
A Classic Christmas (November 16, 2019) as Herself.

Radio

Lux Radio Theater: "Mother Wore Tights" (January 4, 1955) as Myrtle McKinley.

Podcast

Maltin on Movies (February 1, 2019) as Herself.

Recordings

Golden Girl (1951) Soundtrack.
There's No Business Like Show Business (1954) Soundtrack.
Anything Goes (1956) Soundtrack.
Les Girls (1957) Soundtrack.
South Pacific (1958) Soundtrack.
Mitzi (1959).
Mitzi Gaynor Sings the Lyrics of Ira Gershwin (1959).
Happy Anniversary (1959).
Mitzi ... Zings into spring (1977)

Bibliography

Abel. "Film Reviews: South Pacific." *Variety.* March 26, 1958. Retrieved March 26, 2023, from http://www.variety.com.
_____. "Film Reviews: There's No Business Like Show Business." *Variety.* December 8, 1954. Retrieved March 4, 2023, from http://www.variety.com.
Albert, Katherine. "Hollywood's Young Unmarrieds." *Photoplay.* June 1951: 44–47, 75–79.
Allessandrini, Gerard, and Chapin, Ted. *South Pacific* 2-Disc Special Edition DVD Audio Commentary. 20th Century Fox Home Entertainment, 2008.
Arnold, Jeremy. "Article: The I Don't Care Girl On DVD." *Turner Classic Movies.* May 10, 2013. Retrieved February 26, 2023, from http://www.tcm.com.
Arnold, Maxine. "The strange romance of Mitzi Gaynor." *Photoplay.* October 1952: 48–49, 108–111.
Ash, Agnes. "GOLD COAST AGLOW." *The New York Times.* November 4, 1962. Retrieved April 8, 2023, from http://www.nytimes.com.
Atkinson, Brooks. "At The Theatre." *The New York Times.* April 23, 1949. Retrieved January 26, 2023, from http://www.nytimes.com.
Barnes, Mike, and Byrge, Duane. "Mitzi Gaynor, Showbiz Dynamo and Star of 'South Pacific,' Dies at 93." *The Hollywood Reporter.* October 17, 2024. Retrieved October 19, 2024 from http://www.hollywoodreporter.com.
Barrios, Richard. *South Pacific* 2-Disc Special Edition DVD Road Show Version Audio Commentary. 20th Century Fox Home Entertainment, 2008.
Bartlett, Rhett. "Leslie Phillips." *The Hollywood Reporter.* November 8, 2022. Retrieved April 16, 2023, from http://www.hollywoodreporter.com.
Basinger, Jeanine. *Gene Kelly. Pyramid Illustrated History of the Movies.* New York: Pyramid, 1976.
_____. *The Movie Musical!* New York: Knopf, 2019.
Beale, Lauren. "Actress Mitzi Gaynor sells her home." *Los Angeles Times.* January 7, 2014. Retrieved April 22, 2023, from http://www.latimes.com.
Bean, Jack. "My Girl Mitzi by her husband." *Picturegoer.* June 4, 1955: 14–15.
_____. "My Princess Yum Yum." *Photoplay.* August 1956: 50, 101-104.
Bergan, Ronald. *The United Artists Story.* London: Octopus Books, 1986.
Billman, Larry. *Betty Grable: A Bio-Bibliography.* Westport, CT: Greenwood Press, 1993.
Bookbinder, Robert. *The Films of Bing Crosby.* Secaucus, NJ: Citadel Press, 1977.
Brady, Thomas F. "BANK ..." *The New York Times.* May 9, 1951. Retrieved February 10, 2023, from http://www.nytimes.com.
_____. "COLUMBIA ..." *The New York Times.* March 6, 1951. Retrieved February 10, 2023, from http://www.nytimes.com.
_____. "FOX STUDIO ..." *The New York Times.* June 20, 1951. Retrieved February 15, 2023, from http://www.nytimes.com.

Bibliography

———. "JUNE HAVER DRAWS SUSPENSION AT FOX..." *The New York Times*. December 30, 1950. Retrieved February 5, 2023, from http://www.nytimes.com.

Brozan, Nadine. "CHRONICLE." *The New York Times*. April 16, 1997. Retrieved April 17, 2023, from http://www.nytimes.com.

Bruno, Katie. "Mitzi Gaynor. Still a Dynamo at 88." *Closer Weekly*. September 30, 2019: 44–45.

Bunce, Donna. "American Celebration." *The Orange County Register*. November 11, 2009. Retrieved April 18, 2023, from http://www.ocregister.com.

Burns, Kevin. *Betty Grable: Behind the Pin-Up*. Van Ness Films/Foxstar Productions/Twentieth Television/A&E Network/Twentieth Century Fox Film Corporation, 1995.

Calta, Louis. "New 'Zeigfeld Follies.'" *The New York Times*. January 12, 1956. Retrieved March 14, 2023, from http://www.nytimes.com.

———. "'Sally' Revival." *The New York Times*. January 24, 1952. Retrieved February 19, 2023, from http://www.nytimes.com.

Capua, Michelangelo. *Jean Negulesco: The Life and Films*. Jefferson, NC: McFarland, 2017.

———. *Yul Brynner: A Biography*. Jefferson, NC: McFarland, 2014.

Chandler, Charlotte. *Nobody's Perfect: Billy Wilder. A Personal Biography*. Simon & Schuster, 2002.

Christy, George. Untitled. *Beverly Hills Courier*. September 8, 2017: 6.

Clarens, Carlos. *George Cukor*. London: Secker and Warburg [for] the British Film Institute, 1976.

Connolly, Mike. "Impertinent Interview." *Photoplay*, Vol. 45, Iss. 2, 1954: 19–20.

Connor, D. Russell. *Benny Goodman: Listen to His Legacy*. Metuchen, NJ: Scarecrow Press and the Institute of Jazz Studies, 1988.

Corwin, Jane. "Change of Heart." *Photoplay*, January 1953: 68, 78.

Coz, Steve. "*Mitzi Gaynor's Diet & Exercise Secrets*." *National Enquirer*, December 16, 1986: 31.

Crowther, Bosley. "Bloodhounds of Broadway." *The New York Times*. November 15, 1952. Retrieved February 23, 2023, from http://www.nytimes.com.

———. "For Love or Money." *The New York Times*. August 8, 1963. Retrieved April 10, 2023, from http://www.nytimes.com.

———. "The Screen: An Enchanted Evening." *The New York Times*. March 20, 1958. Retrieved March 26, 2023, from http://www.nytimes.com.

———. "The Screen: 'Happy Anniversary.'" *The New York Times*. November 11, 1959. Retrieved April 1, 2023, from http://www.nytimes.com.

———. "THE SCREEN IN REVIEW." *The New York Times*. September 16, 1950. Retrieved January 26, 2023, from http://www.nytimes.com.

———. "THE SCREEN IN REVIEW." *The New York Times*. July 19, 1951. Retrieved February 5, 2023, from http://www.nytimes.com.

———. "The Screen: 'Les Girls.'" *The New York Times*. October 4, 1957. Retrieved March 21, 2023, from http://www.nytimes.com.

———. "The Screen: Two New Films on Local Scene." *The New York Times*. November 21, 1951. Retrieved February 14, 2023, from http://www.nytimes.com.

———. "Screen: 'Surprise Package.'" *The New York Times*. October 15, 1960. Retrieved April 5, 2023, from http://www.nytimes.com.

———. "There's No Business." *The New York Times*. December 17, 1954. Retrieved March 4, 2023, from http://www.nytimes.com.

———. "'...We're Not Married.'" *The New York Times*. July 12, 1952. Retrieved February 19, 2023, from http://www.nytimes.com.

David, Mark. "End of Week Pick Up Sticks: Mitzi Gaynor." *Dirt*. September 20, 2013. Retrieved May 2, 2023, from http://www.dirt.com.

Day, Barry. *Coward on Film: The Cinema of Noël Coward*. Lanham, MD: Scarecrow Press, 2005.

Bibliography

DeCaro, Frank. "The Marvelous Mr. Mackie." *The New York Times.* December 1, 2018. Retrieved April 17, 2023, from http://www.nytimes.com.

Denette, Kelsey. "Reagle Music Theatre." *broadwayWorld.* December 16, 2011. Retrieved April 16, 2023, from http://www.broadwayworld.com.

Diamond, Robert. "Mitzi Gaynor to Be Honored." *broadwayWorld.* February 20, 2009. Retrieved April 16, 2023, from http://www.broadwayworld.com.

Digrazia, Christine. "Finding Duty and Privilege." *The New York Times.* November 11, 2001. Retrieved April 17, 2023, from http://www.nytimes.com.

Duke, Patty, and Jankowski, William J. *In the Presence of Greatness: My Sixty-Year Journey as an Actress.* Albany, GA: BearManor Media, 2018.

_____, and Turan, Kenneth. *Call Me Anna: The Autobiography of Patty Duke.* New York: Bantam Books, 1987.

Eames, John Douglas. *The MGM Story: The Complete History of Fifty Roaring Years.* New York: Crown, 1975.

_____. *The Paramount Story: The Complete History of the Studio and Its 2,805 Films.* London: Octopus Books, 1985.

Emmett, Robert. "Pandemonium Reigned In Paradise." *Photoplay,* June 1955: 60–61, 98–100.

Esterow, Milton. "HOTELS BATTLING." *The New York Times.* October 6, 1962. Retrieved April 8, 2023, from http://www.nytimes.com.

Feinberg, Scott. "TCM Classic Film Fest: Mitzi." *The Hollywood Reporter.* April 26, 2013. Retrieved April 16, 2023, from http://www.hollywoodreporteer.com.

Fendalman, Adam. "Interview: Mitzi Gaynor Lights." *HollywoodChicago.* April 26, 2013. Retrieved April 16, 2023, from http://www.hollywoodchicago.com.

_____. "'South Pacific' with Mitzi." *HollywoodChicago.* March 16, 2013. Retrieved April 16, 2023, from http://www.hollywoodchicago.com.

Finlayson, John. "Mitzi Gets Into the Beatles Act." *Journal American TV magazine.* February 1964.

Fitzgerald, Peter. *Cole Porter in Hollywood: Ca C'est L'Amour.* Turner Entertainment Co./Fitz Film Inc., 2003.

Flinn, Caryl. *Brass Diva: The Life and Legends of Ethel Merman.* Berkeley: University of California Press, 2007.

Foster, Tom. "The Storied Career of Mitzi Gaynor." *tvovermind.* September 1, 2018. Retrieved April 16, 2023, from http://www.tvovermind.com.

Fraser, C. Gerald. "$2 Million in Olympic Lottery." *The New York Times.* July 16, 1978. Retrieved April 18, 2023, from http://www.nytimes.com.

Friedfeld, Eddie. "...MITZI GAYNOR RECALLS 'South Pacific.'" *Cinema Retro.* April 12, 2009. Retrieved March 17, 2023, from http://www.cinemaretro.com.

Fristoe, Roger. "Article: The I Don't Care Girl." *Turner Classic Movies.* March 8, 2014. Retrieved February 26, 2023, from http://www.tcm.com.

_____. "Article: There's No Business Like Show Business." *Turner Classic Movies.* September 19, 2011. Retrieved March 4, 2023, from http://www.tcm.com.

Funke, Lewis. "NEWS AND GOSSIP GATHERED ON THE RIALTO." *The New York Times.* August 24, 1952. Retrieved February 26, 2023, from http://www.nytimes.com.

Gaffney, Dennis. *Joe Directs Marilyn's Funeral.* PBS. Undated. Retrieved April 8, 2023, from http://www.pbs.org.

Garbarini, Todd. "An Evening with Mitzi Gaynor." *Cinemaretro.* November 24, 2014. Retrieved April 16, 2023, from http:///www.Cinemaretro.com.

Gargiulo, Suzanne. *Hans Conried: A Biography; With a Filmography and a Listing of Radio, Television, Stage and Voice Work.* Jefferson, NC: McFarland, 2002.

Gates, Anita. "Mitzi Gaynor, Leading Lady of Movie Musicals, Is Dead at 93." *The New York Times.* October 17, 2024. Retrieved October 19, 2024 from https://www.nytimes.com.

Bibliography

Gaynor, Mitzi. "Kirk Douglas' Former Co-Star, Mitzi Gaynor, on How He Was Always 'the Ragman's Son.'" *Variety*. February 12, 2020. Retrieved April 10, 2023, from http://www.variety.com.

———. "Mitzi Gaynor Remembers." *The Hollywood Reporter*. March 26, 2017. Retrieved April 23, 2023, from http://www.hollywoodreporter.com.

———. "Mitzi Gaynor's Golden Memories of Stanley Donen." *Time*. February 28, 2019. Retrieved April 23, 2023, from http://www.time.com.

Gelb, Arthur. "ROLES IN 'FOLLIES.'" *The New York Times*. July 26, 1955. Retrieved March 11, 2023, from http://www.nytimes.com.

———. "2 New Musicals Advancing Plans." *The New York Times*. November 25, 1955. Retrieved March 14, 2023, from http://www.nytimes.com.

Gene. "The Joker Is Wild." *Variety*. August 27, 1957. Retrieved March 17, 2023, from http://www.variety.com.

Gent, George. "Movies and Variety Shows ... Next Season." *The New York Times*. June 5, 1968. Retrieved April 12, 2023, from http://www.nytimes.com.

Genzlinger, Neil. "TV Christmas Specials." *The New York Times*. December 3, 2015. Retrieved April 11, 2023, from http://www.nytimes.com.

Gould, Jack. "TV: Jack Benny Special." *The New York Times*. March 19, 1959. Retrieved March 28, 2023, from http://www.nytimes.com.

Gould, Jonathan. *Can't Buy Me Love: The Beatles, Britain And America*. New York: Harmony Books, 2007.

Gow, Gordon. *Hollywood in the Fifties*. The International Film Series. New York: A.S. Barnes & Co., and London: A. Zwemmer Ltd., 1971.

Grossberg, Michael. "Touring 'Anything' goes dim." *The Columbus Dispatch*. January 18, 1990: 6.

Hanna, Beth. "2013 TCM Classic Film Festival Announces." *IndieWire*. February 20, 2013. Retrieved April 16, 2023, from http://www.indiewire.com.

Hannett, Michelle. "Hollywood Home Movies." *we are movie geeks*. October 2, 2013. Retrieved April 16, 2023, from http://www.wearemoviegeeks.com.

Harris, Marlys J. *The Zanucks of Hollywood: The Dark Legacy of An American Dynasty*. New York: Crown, 1989.

Hernandez, Greg. "Rita Moreno." *Hollywoodnews*. January 16, 2011. Retrieved April 16, 2023, from http://www.hollywoodnews.com.

Hetrick, Adam. "Film Remake of South Pacific in Development." *Playbill*. July 8, 2010. Retrieved March 27, 2023, from http://www.playbill.com.

H.H.T. "Musical Romp Opens at the Palace." *The New York Times*. June 13, 1953. Retrieved February 9, 2023, from http://www.nytimes.com.

Higham, Charles. *Howard Hughes: The Secret Life*. New York: Putnam, 1993.

Hirschhorn, Clive. *The Columbia Story*. London: Pyramid Books, 1989.

———. *The Universal Story. The Complete History of the Studio and All Its Films*. London: Octopus Books, 1983.

Hoey, Michael A. *ELVIS' FAVORITE DIRECTOR: The Amazing 52-Year Career of Norman Taurog*. Duncan, OK: BearManor Media, 2014.

Holden, Stephen. "Landing in New York." *The New York Times*. May 19, 2010. Retrieved April 17, 2023, from http://www.nytimes.com.

———. "STAGE.'" *The New York Times*. November 2, 1986. Retrieved April 17, 2023, from http://www.nytimes.com.

Jessel, George, with Austin, John. *The World I Lived*. Chicago: Regnery, 1975.

Johnson, Hildegarde. "Who's telling the truth?" *Photoplay*. January 1958: 46–47, 80.

Jordan, Neil, and Murphy, Cillian. *Breakfast On Pluto* DVD Audio Commentary. Sony Pictures Home Entertainment, 2006.

Judge, Frank. "Danny Thomas Fills MGM Sets With Swingers." *Boston Sunday Herald TV Magazine*. February 6, 1966.

Bibliography

_____. "Two-Point Gal in Vegas." *The Sunday Star TV ,agazine.* October 13–19, 1968: 3–4.
Kael, Pauline. *5001 Nights at the Movies.* New York: Holt, Rinehart and Winston, 1984.
Kahn Atkins, Irene. *Henry Koste: A Director's Guild Oral History.* Metuchen, NJ: Scarecrow Press, 1987.
Kaplan, James. *Sinatra: The Chairman.* New York: Doubleday, 2015.
Karen, Paul. "Doc sings Newman's song." *Variety.* October 23, 1997. Retrieved April 21, 2023, from http://www.variety.com.
Kashner, Sam, and Schoenberger, Nancy. *A Talent for Genius: The Life and Times of Oscar Levant.* New York: Villard Books, 1994.
Kaufman, David. *Doris Day: The Untold Story of the Girl Next Door.* New York: Virgin Books USA, 2008.
_____. *Some Enchanted Evenings: The Glittering Life and Times of Mary Martin.* New York: St. Martin's Press, 2016.
Kaufman Feder, Karen. "Mitzi Gaynor..." *Palos Verdes Pulse.* September 13, 2020. Retrieved April 28, 2023, from http://www.palosverdespulse.com.
Kellow, Brian. *Ethel Merman.* New York: Viking, 2007.
Kennedy, Matthew. *Edmund Goulding's Dark Victory: Hollywood's Genius Bad Boy.* Madison: University of Wisconsin Press, 2004.
_____. *Roadshow! The Fall of Film Musicals in the 1960s.* New York: Oxford University Press, 2015.
King, Susan. "'Oscar Hammerstein II: Out of My Dreams" *Los Angeles Times.* March 7, 2012. Retrieved April 22, 2023, from http://www.latimes.com.
Kobal, John. *Gotta Sing, Gotta Dance: A Pictorial History of Film Musicals.* Feltham, NY: Hamlyn, 1970.
Kourlas, Gia. "Lara Spencer Apologizes." *The New York Times.* August 26, 2019. Retrieved April 17, 2023, from http://www.nytimes.com.
Krebs, Alvin. "Notes on People." *The New York Times.* August 6, 1974. Retrieved April 15, 2023, from http://www.nytimes.com.
_____, and Thomas, Jr., Robert Mcg. "Notes on People." *The New York Times.* April 1, 1982. Retrieved April 18, 2023, from http://www.nytimes.com.
Lambert, Molly. "...Plot of Land in Los Angeles." *The New York Times.* August 23, 2019. Retrieved April 17, 2023, from http://www.nytimes.com.
Lentz, Robert J. *Lee Marvin: His Films and Career.* Jefferson, NC: McFarland, 2000.
Lev, Peter. *Twentieth Century-Fox: The Zanuck-Skouras Years, 1935–1965.* Austin: University of Texas Press, 2013.
Levy, Emanuel. *George Cukor: Master of Elegance: Hollywood's Legendary Director And His Stars.* New York: Morrow, 1994.
Lewis, Jessica. "Gaines, Jackson, Plimpton et al. to Present..." *broadwayWorld.* April 28, 2010. Retrieved April 16, 2023, from http://www.broadwayworld.com.
LoBianco, Lorraine. "Article: For Love or Money." *Turner Classic Movies.* June 17, 2014. Retrieved April 10, 2023, from http://www.tcm.com.
_____. "Article: Golden Girl." *Turner Classic Movies.* January 24, 2011. Retrieved February 14, 2023, from http://www.tcm.com.
Logan, Joshua. *Movie Stars, Real People, and Me.* New York: Dell, 1979.
Lyons, Shelley. *Hidden Hollywood: Treasures From the 20th Century Fox Vaults.* Foxstar Productions/Fox Television Studios/Van Ness Films/American Movie Classics, 1999.
Marsh, Robb. "Mitzi Gaynor. A Celebration. Part 1." *Films of the Golden Age.* Fall 2001: 36–49.
_____. "Mitzi Gaynor. A Celebration. Part 2." *Films of the Golden Age.* Winter 2001/2002: 32–47.
McAdoo, Mandy. "Reel Life: Marilyn Monroe." *Reelzchannel.* August 3, 2012. Retrieved April 16, 2023, from http://www.reelzchannel.com.

Bibliography

McFadden, Robert D. "Donald W. Duncan ... Is Dead." *The New York Times*. May 6, 2016. Retrieved January 24, 2023, from http://www.nytimes.com.

McGee, Gary. *Doris Day: Sentimental Journey*. Jefferson, NC: McFarland, 2005.

McGee, Tom. *The Girl with the Million Dollar Legs: Betty Grable*. New York: Vestal Press, 1994.

Merman, Ethel, with Eells, George. *Merman: An Autobiography*. New York: Berkley, 1979.

Miller, Frank. "Article: Les Girls." *Turner Classic Movies*. April 20, 2005. Retrieved March 21, 2023, from http:///www.tcm.com.

———. "Article: South Pacific." *Turner Classic Movies*. February 27, 2003. Retrieved March 27, 2023, from http://www.tcm.com.

———. "Article: Take Care of My Little Girl." *Turner Classic Movies*. June 6, 2013. Retrieved February 5, 2023, from http://www.tcm.com.

Montgomery, Steve. "Satellite Awards Nominations." *Alt Film Guide*. December 2, 2011. Retrieved April 16, 2023, from http:///www.altfg.com.

Morris, Bernadine. "RESORT WEAR." *The New York Times*. August 10, 1982. Retrieved April 17, 2023, from http://www.nytimes.com.

Muller, Eddie. *Dark City Dames: The Wicked Women of Film Noir*. New York: Regan Books, 2001.

Nason, Richard W. "'ANNIVERSARY WALTZ' IN NEW TEMPO." *The New York Times*. May 10, 1959. Retrieved April 1, 2023, from http://www.nytimes.com.

Noan, Frederick. *The Sound of Their Music: The Story of Rodgers & Hammerstein*. New York: Applause Theatre & Cinema Books, 2002.

Nolan, Scott Allen. *The Cinema of Sinatra: The Actor, on Screen and in Song*. Lowell, MA: Midnight Marquee Press, 2008.

O.A.G. "Palace Begins Run of 'Three Young Texans.'" *The New York Times*. April 17, 1954. Retrieved March 1, 2023, from http://www.nytimes.com.

O'Connor, John J. "TV.'" *The New York Times*. March 13, 1976. Retrieved April 16, 2023, from http://www.nytimes.com.

———. "TV." *The New York Times*. March 28, 1977. Retrieved April 17, 2023, from http://www.nytimes.com.

Page, Patti, with Press, Skip. *This Is My Song: A Memoir*. Bath, NH: Kathdan Books, 2009.

Parish, James Robert, and Pitts, Michael R. *Hollywood Songsters: Singers Who Could Act and Actors Who Sing. Volume 2. A Biographical Dictionary*. New York: Routledge, 2003.

Pastos, Spero. *Pin-Up: The Tragedy of Betty Grable*. New York: Putnam, 1986.

Peck, Seymour. "More Enchanted Evenings." *The New York Times*. September 1, 1957. Retrieved March 27, 2023, from http://www.nytimes.com.

Pedelty, Donovan. "The Biggest Name of 1958." *Picturegoer*. December 28, 1957: 8–9.

———. "The Biggest Name of 1958. Part II." *Picturegoer*. January 4, 1958: 10–11.

———. "The Man Behind That Gaynor Sparkle." *Picturegoer*. January 11, 1958: 16–17.

Peterson, Tyler. "92Y's LYRICS & LYRICISTS 2015." *broadwayWorld*. October 28, 2014. Retrieved April 16, 2023, from http://www.broadwayworld.com.

Pfeiffer, Lee. "BOOK REVIEW: "STARRING THE PLAZA." *Cinemretro*. September 9, 2017. Retrieved April 16, 2023, from http://www.cinemaretro.com.

Pianne, Charlie. "Rivera Honored." *broadwayWorld*. June 3, 2009. Retrieved April 16, 2023, from http://www.broadwayworld.com.

Portantiere, Michael. "The Cockeyed Optimism of Mitzi Gaynor." *Life After 50*. December 2012: 12–16.

Porter, Darwin. *Howard Hughes: Hell's Angel. America's Notorious Bisexual Billionaire*. New York: Blood Moon, 2005.

Prelutsky, Burt. "Mitzi Keeps It Light." *TV Guide*. October 1968: 12–15.

Price, Betsy. "Stage legend Mitzi Gaynor dishes." *USA Today*. February 19, 2013. Retrieved April 22, 2023, from http://www.usatoday.com.

Bibliography

Pryor, Thomas M. "BEN HECHT...." *The New York Times.* August 22, 1951. Retrieved February 15, 2023, from http://www.nytimes.com.

———. "BY WAY OF REPORT." *The New York Times.* January 25, 1959. Retrieved March 27, 2023, from http://www.nytimes.com.

———. "Came the Hollywood Dawn." *The New York Times.* January 26, 1958. Retrieved March 27, 2023, from http://www.nytimes.com.

———. "...Gene Kelly Takes Over." *The New York Times.* May 1, 1957. Retrieved March 20, 2023, from http://www.nytimes.com.

———. "HOLLYWOOD JOTTINGS." *The New York Times.* October 14, 1951. Retrieved February 16, 2023, from http://www.nytimes.com.

———. "KRAMER ..." *The New York Times.* August 16, 1951. Retrieved February 15, 2023, from http://www.nytimes.com.

———. "LAWFORD IS CAST..." *The New York Times.* May 22, 1953. Retrieved February 26, 2023, from http://www.nytimes.com.

———. "MOULIN PRESIDENT..." *The New York Times.* February 23, 1955. Retrieved March 6, 2023, from http://www.nytimes.com.

———. "'... Pacific' Launching." *The New York Times.* August 11, 1957. Retrieved March 27, 2023, from http://www.nytimes.com.

———. "RHONDA FLEMING...." *The New York Times.* April 27, 1955. Retrieved March 11, 2023, from http://www.nytimes.com.

——— "SALLY, IRENE." *The New York Times.* August 7, 1951. Retrieved February 15, 2023, from http://www.nytimes.com.

———. "TODON..." *New York Times.* May 14, 1956. Retrieved March 14, 2023, from http://www.nytimes.com.

———. "26 Stars." *The New York Times.* January 30, 1958. Retrieved March 27, 2023, from http://www.nytimes.com.

———. "WANGER CHANGES..." *The New York Times.* December 23, 1954. Retrieved March 6, 2023, from http://www.nytimes.com.

Raines, Halsey. "FILM 'PACKAGE' ON A GRECIAN ISLE." *The New York Times.* November 8, 1959. Retrieved April 3, 2023, from http://www.nytimes.com.

Roberts, Eleanor. "Mitzi Gaynor's nostalgic about 'South Pacific.'" *Sunday Herald Traveller TV Magazine.* November 21–27, 1971: 4–5.

Roberts, Wynn. "Her Happiness is Showing." *Photoplay.* July 1953: 58, 104–107.

Robertson, Nan. "'Oscar' Fete Is Big One for Fashion." *The New York Times.* April 7, 1959. Retrieved April 1, 2023, from http://www.nytimes.com.

Robertson, Susan. *Bucking Hollywood.* Conneaut Lake, PA: Page Publishing, 2019.

Rosen, Richard. "THEATER; Playbill Biographies." *The New York Times.* June 16, 1991. Retrieved April 17, 2023, from http://www.nytimes.com.

Rosley, Nicole. "Oscar Hammerstein Tribute." *broadwayWorld.* January 18, 2012. Retrieved April 16, 2023, from http://www.broadwayworld.com.

Salamon, Julie. "TELEVISION REVIEW." *The New York Times.* March 26, 2001. Retrieved April 17, 2023, from http://www.nytimes.com.

Santopietro, Tom. *Considering Doris Day: A Biography.* New York: Thomas Dunne Books, 2007.

Schechter, Scott. *Judy Garland: The Day-by-Day Chronicle of a Legend.* Lanham, MD: First Taylor Trade, 2002.

Sennett, Shae. "Some Like It Hot Role." *SlashFilm.* August 8, 2022. Retrieved April 16, 2023, from https://www.slashfilm.com.

Shanley, John P. "Donald O'Connor..." *The New York Times.* October 12, 1960. Retrieved April 6, 2023, from http://www.nytimes.com.

Shemanski, Frances. "Summer Theater Straw Hat Directory." *The New York Times.* June 20, 1976. Retrieved April 17, 2023, from http://www.nytimes.com.

Bibliography

Shepard, Richard F. "'Big' Names at President's Show." *The New York Times.* May 23, 1964. Retrieved April 11, 2023, from http://www.nytimes.com.

———. "...Sinatra Show." *The New York Times.* October 20, 1959. Retrieved April 2, 2023, from http:///www.nytimes.com.

Sherman, Robert. "Music." *The New York Times.* May 13, 1990. Retrieved April 17, 2023, from http://www.nytimes.com.

Shevey, Sandra. *The Marilyn Scandal: Her True Life Revealed by Those Who Knew Her.* New York: William Morrow, 1988.

Shipman, David. *The Great Movie Stars—The International Years.* London: Angus and Robertson, 1972.

Sibley, John. "$100,000 WINNERS PICKED IN LOTTERY." *The New York Times.* October 20, 1967. Retrieved April 11, 2023, from http://www.nytimes.com.

Sidney, Robert. *With Malice Towards Some: Tales from a Life Dancing with the Stars.* 1st Books, 2003.

Sierra, Gabriella. "Photo Flash: LA Premiere." *broadwayWorld.* February 3, 2009. Retrieved April 16, 2023, from http://www.broadwayworld.com.

Sikov, Ed. *On Sunset Boulevard: The Life and Times of Billy Wilder.* New York: Hyperion, 1998.

Silverman, Stephen M. *Dancing on the Ceiling: Stanley Donen and His Movies.* New York: Knopf, 1996.

Smith, Jeremy. "Some Like It Hot." *SlashFilm.* January 22, 2023. Retrieved April 16, 2023, from http://www.slashfilm.com.

Soares, Andy. "Mitzi Gaynor at South Pacific Academy Screening." *AltFilm Guide.* June 26, 2010. Retrieved April 16, 2023, from http://www.altfg.com.

Solloway, Lary. "STARS OVER MIAMI." *The New York Times.* December 3, 1961. Retrieved April 6, 2023, from http://www.nytimes.com.

Solomon, Aubrey. *Twentieth Century-Fox: A Corporate and Financial History.* Lanham, MD: Scarecrow Press, 1988.

Solomon, Aubrey, and Thomas, Tony. *The Films of 20th Century Fox: A Pictorial History.* Secaucus, NJ: Citadel Press, 1979.

Stafford, Jeff. "Article: The Joker Is Wild." *Turner Classic Movies.* November 22, 2005. Retrieved March 17, 2023, from http://www.tcm.com.

Sterritt, David. "Article: My Blue Heaven." *Turner Classic Movies.* November 28, 2011. Retrieved January 26, 2023, from http://www.tcm.com.

Stoddard, Sarah. "Mitzi Gets Slinky And How." *Picturegoer.* June 16, 1956: 12–13.

Swanson, Pauline. "Mitzi Made Her Mind Up." *Photoplay.* December 1954: 60–61, 84.

Thomas, Bob. *I Got Rhythm! The Ethel Merman Story.* New York: Putnam's, 1985.

Thomas, Tony. *The Films of Gene Kelly: Song And Dance Man.* Secaucus, NJ: Citadel Press, 1974.

———. *Howard Hughes in Hollywood.* Secaucus, NJ: Citadel Press, 1985.

Thompson, Charles. *The Complete Crosby.* London: Allen, 1978.

Thompson, Howard. "TV." *The New York Times.* March 28, 1973. Retrieved April 14, 2023, from http://www.mytimes.com.

———. "TV: 2 C.B.S. Surprises." *The New York Times.* February 4, 1974. Retrieved April 15, 2023, from http:///www.nytimes.com.

Thomson, David. *"Have You Seen?" A Personal Introduction to 1,000 Films.* New York: Knopf, 2008.

Tough, Paul. "This You Call a College?" *The New York Times.* February 15, 2004. Retrieved April 17, 2023, from http://www.nytimes.com.

Varley, Eddie. "Mitzi Gaynor Celebrates SOUTH PACIFIC." *broadwayWorld.* May 5, 2009. Retrieved April 16, 2023, from http://www.broadwayworld.com.

———. "MY LIFE BEHIND THE SEQUINS." *broadwayWorld.* February 24, 2009. Retrieved April 22, 2023, from http://www.broadwayworld.com.

Bibliography

Viens, Stephen. "Health Shock for Mitzi Gaynor." *Star*. September 15, 1998: 8.
Vlastnik, Frank, and Ross, Laura. *The Art of Bob Mackie*. New York: Simon & Schuster, 2021.
Vogel, Michelle. *Marilyn Monroe: Her Films, Her Life*. Jefferson, NC: McFarland, 2014.
Ward, Alan. "Mitzi Gaynor: Fond Memories Of Nellie Forebush." *The Sunday Tribune Entertainment Week*. August 20, 1967.
Warren, Doug. *Betty Grable: The Reluctant Movie Queen*. Crossroad Press, 2016.
Weiler, A.H. "BY WAY OF REPORT." *The New York Times*. November 25, 1951. Retrieved February 16, 2023, from http://www.nytimes.com.
_____. "...Passion And Crime." *The New York Times*. October 13, 1957. Retrieved March 27, 2023, from http://www.nytimes.com.
_____. "Screen: ... 'Anything Goes.'" *The New York Times*. March 22, 1956. Retrieved March 11, 2023, from http://www.nytimes.com.
_____. "Screen: 'Birds and Bees.'" *The New York Times*. April 23, 1956. Retrieved March 14, 2023, from http://www.nytimes.com.
Weinraub, Bernard. "Broadway Takes a Detour." *The New York Times*. March 22, 2001. Retrieved April 17, 2023, from http://www.nytimes.com.
_____. "For the Old Hollywood." *The New York Times*. March 30, 2001. Retrieved April 17, 2023, from http://www.nytimes.com.
Weissman, Ginny. "Zing into Spring with Mitzi." *Chicago Tribune TV Week*. March 27–April 2, 1977: 2.
Wicker, Tom. "Johnson, at a Party Salute.'" *The New York Times*. May 26, 1964. Retrieved April 11, 2023, from http://www.nytimes.com.
Wilkins, Barbara. "Mitzi Gaynor. The Star Entertains at Home." *Bon Appetit*. April 1977: 51–52.
Wilson, John S. "THROUGH THE YEARS...." *The New York Times*. October 4, 1959. Retrieved April 1, 2023, from http://www.nytimes.com.
Wilson, Liza. "They Call Her Sparkle Plenty." *Photoplay*. April 1952: 63–65, 99–101.
Witbeck, Charles. "Monday Night AT 10 ON NBC." *Los Angeles Herald-Examiner TV Weekly*. October 13, 1968: 10–11.
Witchell, Alex. "AT HOME WITH: ARNOLD SCAASI." *The New York Times*. October 3, 1996. Retrieved April 17, 2023, from http://www.nytimes.com.
York, Carl. "Gossip of Hollywood." *Photoplay*. June 1955; 36.
_____. "Gossip of Hollywood." *Photoplay*. July 1955: 30–31.
Zolotow, Sam. "MARLOWE DRAMA ..." *The New York Times*. January 2, 1956. Retrieved March 14, 2023, from http://www.nytimes.com.
_____. "NEW PRODUCTION OF 'FLAHOOLEY' SET." *The New York Times*. March 14, 1952. Retrieved February 20, 2023, from http://www.nytimes.com.
_____. "ROONEY TO APPEAR..." *The New York Times*. May 22, 1953. Retrieved February 26, 2023, from http://www.nytimes.com.
_____. "2D SHOW IS DUE ON PEACE CORPS." *The New York Times*. March 21, 1962. Retrieved April 7, 2023, from http://www.nytimes.com.

Index

Numbers in **_bold italics_** indicate pages with illustrations

Adler, Buddy 77, 88
Albertson, Jack 114–115
All About Alfred 134
Allyson, June 1, 82
American Movie Classics "Comedy Classics" 132
Andrews, Julie 141
Anything Goes (film) 2, 3, 56–**_59_**, 60, 148
Anything Goes (stage show) 131–**_133_**
Arno, Sig 14–15

Bacon, Lloyd 28–29, 31–32
Baird, Sharon 35–37
Ball, Lucille 107–108
Bean, Jack 3–4, 17, 42–46, 48–52, 54–57, 60–**_65_**, 67–68, 73, 78–79, 87–91, 94–97, 99, 101, 104–105, 111, 119, 122, 126–127, 129–131, 134, 136, 142, 143
The Beatles 4, 94–95, 147
Bedtime Story 91–92
Benny, Jack 81
Berlin, Irving 15, 47, 82, 85, 105, 109, 115, 130, 146
Berry, Ken 109–111, 117–118
Biography (TV show) 134–135
The Birds and the Bees 2, 60–61, 83
The Bob Braun Show 127
The Bob Hope Special 104, 106
Bracken, Eddie 34, 41, 134
Brady, Scott 35–37
Brando, Marlon 68, 92
Brazzi, Rossano 74–75, 77–78, 88, 129, 148
Breakfast on Pluto 134–136
Bronbadt, Aida 13–15
Brynner, Yul 85

Camelot (film) 96
Can-Can (film) 59
Carlino, Tom 95, 101, 134–135
Caron, Leslie 30, 62, 145
Carson, Johnny 108
Castle, Nick 57, 60
Cavalcade of Champions 108
CBS News Sunday Morning 147
Charisse, Cyd 11, 13, 69
Charmoli, Tony 5, 111, 112, 114–115, 117–121, 123, 125, 134, 136–137
The Children of Lindos 86
Cinema Showcase 127–128
Civic Light Opera Association 2, 14–18, 34–35, 39
Clark, Roy 120–121
A Classic Christmas 147
Colbert, Claudette 8
Cole, Jack 31–32, 39, 41, 47, 69, 71
Como, Perry 107–108
Connors, Mike 109–111
Cover Girl 101, 103
Coward, Noël 85–86, 128, 132
Coyle, Richard Brown 17, **_18_**, 38, 40–41, 148
Crain, Jeanne 26
Crawford, Joan 19
Crosby, Bing 56, 58, 84–85, 135
Cukor, George 69, 71–72, 132, 134
Cusack, Philip 131

Dailey, Dan 22–**_23_**, 24–25, 47, 109–111
Damn Yankees (stage show) 55–56
Damon Runyon's Bloodhounds of Broadway 35–**_36_**, 37, 41
Daniels, Danny 105
Danny Thomas Special: My Home Town 96

165

Index

Day, Dennis 28–29
Day, Doris 3, 67, 83, 101
DeHaven, Gloria 27, 30
The Dick Clark Show 86
Dietrich, Marlene 7, 121
DiMaggio, Joe 48, 92
Dolan, Anton 12, 14
Donen, Stanley 85–86
Douglas, Kirk 91–*93*, 147
Down Among the Sheltering Palms 26–*28*, 78
Downey, Robert, Jr. 141–142
Dream Girl: The Making of Marilyn Monroe 148
Duke, Patty 84
Dunlap, Richard 105–106
Durante, Jimmy 85

The Ed Sullivan Show 3–4, 62, 93–95, 147
Elg, Taina 69, 71–73
Etienne, Kathryn 11, *13*

The Fabulous Fox 135
Feder, Karen Kaufman 130–131
Feinstein, Michael 143, 146–148
Felix, Seymour 26, 29, 31–32
Flatt, Ernie 57, 97
For Love or Money 91–*93*, 147
The Frank Sinatra Timex Show 84–85
Funny You Never Knew 147

Gardner, Ava 19
Garland, Judy 37, 62, 74, 82
Gaynor, Janet 21, 30
Gennaro, Peter 99, 101
The George Jessel Show 44
Getting to Know You 127
Les Girls 2, 62, 69–*70*, 71–73, 92, 135–136, 145
Gobel, George 60–61, 147
Golden Girl 2, 17, 21, 25, 27–29, 92, 145
Gone with the Wind 105–106
Good Morning America 136
Goodman, Benny 123, 125
Gordon, Michael 91, *93*
Goulding, Edmund 26, 34
Grable, Betty 10, 17, 22–*23*, 24–25, 29–30, 57, 104, 132
Grahame, Gloria 52
The Great Waltz 15–17, 20
Griffin, Merv 107
The Gypsy Lady 14

Hammerstein, Oscar 52, 67–68, 73, 78, 105, 136, 141
Handley, Alan 82, 88, 96
Happy Anniversary 3, 82–*83*, 84, 118
Haver, June 22, 30, 48
Hayward, Susan 67
The Helen Morgan Story 59
Hello: A Portrait of Leslie Phillips 145
Henie, Sonja 8
Henry, Bob 101, 103
Hepburn, Audrey 67
Here Comes Donald 5, 53, 57, 88
Hollywood, Hollywood (film) 107
The Hollywood Reporter 132, 134, 146, 149
Hope, Bob 81, 104, 106
Hopkins, Linda 118
Hornblow, Arthur, Jr. 74, 77
Horne, Lena 12
Hughes, Howard 4, 41, 43, 68–69, 147
Hunter, Jeffrey 44, 79
Hunter, Ross 86, 107

The I Don't Care Girl 2, 3, 27, 30–*33*, 145
The Interviews: An Oral History of Television 141–142
It's Your Health 5, 17

The Jack Benny Hour 81
Jamboree 53
Jeanmaire 57–58
Jessel, George 17, 19, 21, 25, 28, 30, 35, 37, 44
The Joker Is Wild 2, 3, 64–66, 145
Jollyanna 4, 34, 39–41, 44, 46
Jones, Harmon 35, 37
Jones, Shirley 91, 136
Jordan, Neil 135–136

Kaye, Danny 13
Kelly, Gene 15, 62, 69, 71
Kendall, Kay 69, 71–73
Knight, Ted 111–112
Koster, Henry 17, 19–20, 22, 24
The Kraft Music Hall: "Mitzi Gaynor Christmas Show" 5, 98–100

Landon, Michael 115
Landsberg, Morris 87, 90
Lang, Walter 47, 49
Las Vegas (TV show) 99
Leisen, Mitchell 51
Lester, Edwin 14–17, 19, 34
Levant, Oscar 31–33

Index

Levin, Henry 44
Lewis, Robert 57
Lifestyles of the Rich and Famous 130
Logan, Joshua 66–68, 73–75, 77–79, 132
Louisiana Purchase 15
Lundigan, William 27
Lux Radio Theater 24, 26, 57

Mackie, Bob 4, 96–97, 99, 101, 103–106, 108, 110–111, 114, 117,-18, 121, 125, 127–128, 130–132, 134, 136–138, 148
MacLeod, Gavin 123, 125
Mahoney, Tom 131
Maltin, Leonard 143, 146–147
Maltin on Movies 146–147
Marshall, Herbert 12
Martin, Dean 84–85
Martin, Mary 3, 66–67, 74–75, 78
Martin, Ross 106
McCook, John 123
Melcher, Martin 67, 83
Merman, Ethel 1, 47–50, 55–56, 84, 93, 95, 105–106, 134
The Merv Griffin Show 107
Mia, a Dancer's Journey 145
Miller, David 82
Minnelli, Liza 95
Miranda, Carmen 11, 13
Mitzi (album) 81
Mitzi (TV special) 4, 101–***102***, 103–104, 112
Mitzi ... A Tribute to the American Housewife 111–***113***, 114, 123, 145
Mitzi and 100 Guys 5, 114–***116***, 117
Mitzi Gaynor: Impressions of the Fox Years 137
Mitzi Gaynor Razzle Dazzle!: The Special Years 125, 137, 139
Mitzi Gaynor Sings the Lyrics of Ira Gershwin (album) 81–82
Mitzi...Roarin' in the 20's 117–***119***
Mitzi ... The First Time 4, 109–111
Mitzi ... What's Hot, What's Not 4, 122–***124***, 125
Mitzi Zings into Spring 120–121, 123, 135
Mitzi's 2nd Special 4, 105–***106***, 107
Moffitt, John 110
Monroe, Marilyn 1–3, 25, 43–44, 46–50, 71, 80–81, 92, 141, 148
Moore, Terry 41, 46, 51
Moreno, Rita 136, 140, 148
My Blue Heaven 17, 20, 22, ***23***–25

Naughty Marietta 15, 17–18
Negulesco, Jean 26
The Night They Raided Minsky's 96
The 1974 Annual Las Vegas Entertainment Awards 114
Niven, David 60–61, 81–82, ***83***, 84
North, Sheree 62, 74
Norton, Cliff 111–112

O'Connor, Donald 3, 47–48, 50–53, 56–58, 61, 80, 88, 134, 148
Oklahoma (film) 52
Orbach, Jerry 111–112
Orry-Kelly 69, 72
Osborne, Robert 145–146
Oscar Hammerstein II—Out of My Dreams 141

Pal Joey (film) 59
Pasetta, Marty 107
Passion, Prejudice and South Pacific: Creating an American Masterpiece 138–139
Perry Como's Winter Show 107–198
Peters, Jean 26, 69
Phillips, Leslie 71–72, 145
Pinza, Ezio 66, 75, 106
Pleshette, Suzanne 111–***113***
Porter, Cole 17, 19–20, 57, 69, 93, 120, 123, 131, 147

Ray, Johnnie 47, 50
Razzle Dazzle: My Life Behind the Sequins 4, 138–140, 142–143
Red Carpet Report 143
Reel Life: Marilyn Monroe 141
Reflets de Cannes 62, 80
Reiner, Carl 117–119, 137
Reynolds, Burt 129–130
Reynolds, Debbie 67, 89, 145
Rita Moreno: Just a Girl Who Decided to Go for It 148
Ritchard, Cyril 99–100
Ritter, Thelma 91
Rivera, Chita 138–139
Roberta 14
Robertson, Dale 29, 134
Rodgers, Richard 52, 67–68, 73, 136
Rogers, Ginger 74, 97, 132
Rogers, Wayne 120–121
Rooney, Mickey 43, 139
Rowan & Martin's Laugh-In 104, 106, 117, 123

Index

Sabellico, Richard **133**
Sidney, Robert 37, 41, 81, 89–90, 94–95, 109, 134
Siegel, Sol C. 17, 19–20, 22, 47, 50, 62, 72
Sinatra, Frank 3, 46–47, 58, 64, 66–68, 84–85, 90, 107
The 16th Annual Satellite Awards 140
Some Like It Hot 80
Song of Norway 14–15
Song Without Words: The Life and Times of Peter Ilyich Tchaikovsky 14
South Pacific 1–3, 20, 66, 73–**76**, 77–81, 88, 89, 92, 95, 133, 136, 138–**140**, 143, 146–147, 149
Stanwyck, Barbara 60
A Star Is Born 52, 82
Stern, David 137
Sturges, Preston 60–61
Sullivan, Ed 3–4, 62, 93–96
Surprise Package 85–**87**

Take Care of My Little Girl 26
Tanner, Tony 99–100
Taurog, Norman 60–61
Taylor, Elizabeth 67
TCM A Salute to Mitzi Gaynor 145
There's No Business Like Show Business 1–2, 44, 47–**49**, 50, 52, 54–57, 78, 81, 106, 110, 132, 145
The 30th Annual Academy Awards 79–80
The 31st Annual Academy Awards 5, 82

The 32nd Annual Academy Awards 88
The 33rd Annual Academy Awards 88
The 39th Annual Academy Awards 97
This Is Your Life 88
Thomas, Danny 96
Three Young Texans 2, 44–**45**
The Tonight Show Starring Johnny Carson 108, 114, 120
Turner, Lana 19
The 26th Annual Academy Awards 51
2011 Primetime Creative Arts Emmy Awards 140

Underworld 132–133
Urie, John 101, 103

Vancouver: Focus on Expo 86 128
Van Eyssen, Lisa 137
Verdon, Gwen 31–32, 56
Vidor, Charles 64

Walston, Ray 74–75, 78–79, 134
Wayne, David 19, 23, 31
We're Not Married 34
The Wild One 69, 71
Wilder, Billy 80
Withers, Jane 111–**113**

Zanuck, Darryl F. 21–22, 25, 32, 46
Ziegfeld Follies (stage show) 61–62
Zinnemann, Fred 52

www.ingramcontent.com/pod-product-compliance
Lightning Source LLC
Chambersburg PA
CBHW052100300426
44117CB00013B/2224